# The Unique Factor

David Webb

Printed in the United States of America

First Printing: 2025

Eternal Kingdom International Publishing, LLC

LIBRARY OF CONGRESS

LCCN: 2025947844

ISBN- 978-1-968815-03-5 - Paperback

ISBN- 978-1-968815-05-9 - eBook

ISBN- 978-1-968815-04-2 - Hardcover

But ye are a chosen generation, a royal priesthood, an holy nation, a peculiar people; that ye should shew forth the praises of him who hath called you out of darkness into his marvelous light.

- Ephesians 2:10 (KJV)

# Dedication:

I dedicate this book to the faithful voices—my friends and mentors—who urged me to write, who believed there was a message worth preserving in ink. I dedicate it also to my children and grandchildren, that they may one day read and walk in the inheritance of these words.

I dedicate it to my Pastor, whose request stirred me to begin. For though this book now stands complete, other manuscripts have been assembled quietly in the background over the years, waiting for their appointed time, fulfilling the charge laid upon me.

David Webb

# Foreword

## *By Adam Bradford,*

Throughout history, Jewish sages would remind their students that there were "no such thing as coincidences", and that everything had it's reason woven into the divine purpose and design of God. After my first encounter with the author, which was on a professional level due to the nature of our work, I learned that David was a teacher and a writer of faith-based books. This acknowledgement of his accomplishments didn't come by casual conversation; it came by a test that David was enduring at the moment, a trial of a life-threatening physical ailment that had attacked his body. Within our conversations that ensued the crisis of his ordeal, our identities through the Messiah were revealed to one another.

Identity. It is the status byword, the mantra of today's current culture; to identify and to be identified by the social norms of a society searching for affirmations and absolutes in an abyss of disproportioned reality with no real answers. As the Word of God states in 1st Corinthians 14:33, "For God is not the author of confusion but of peace….", the understanding of our identity that comes from the Author of our true nature is the missing piece of the puzzle, the antagonist that dispels the confusion and the lies we have been hypnotized and brainwashed into believing that we are much less than what His perfect purpose is for us. David's book admonishes on the freedom and the power of knowing the 'real' you that was ordained before the beginning of time as we know it, an identity birthed in the royalty of Heaven that endows us with inner equipped strengths and capabilities made to perfection in pulling down the strongholds of Hell.

David's book reminds me of the urgency in Mordechai's voice as he addresses his niece Hadassah of the impending doom pronounced on their people, and reminds her of who she was before the status quo gave her the Persian identity of Ester. She was a Jew placed into the palace of a pagan kingdom, and hiding behind a wall of false identity would not save her from Haman's plot of annihilation. In such, the lives of God's people hung in the balance of the identity that God had given her before she was ever born.

During and after reading the work that David has placed together in this book, I can hear the words of Mordechai resounding as he stated, "For if you fail to speak up now, relief and deliverance will come to the Jews from a different direction; but you and your father's family will perish. Who knows whether you didn't come into your royal position precisely for such a time as this?" The Spirit of God has endowed David with such a powerful tool that is quite deadly in smashing down the sacred cows of the misidentification and misunderstanding of our calling and purpose. It is a book written for "such a time as this", one that will challenge the reader with thought-provoking questions yet providing answers that give peace of mind and hope.

Adam Bradford,
> Author of
> The United States of Apostasy
> We Have Seen Them
> Encounters of Destiny
> The Angel's Winepress
> When the Last Cowboy is Gone
> The Law of The Lamb.

# Contents

# Prelude

## *A Voice Is Calling You Out*

You were never meant to blend in. You were never formed to remain hidden in the crowd. Before your mother knew your name, God had written it into a book  - a divine manuscript detailing your design, your gifts, and your impact. *"In the volume of the book it is written of me, I come to do your will, O God"* (Hebrews 10:7; Psalm 40:7). That book exists. And  Heaven will one day compare what you lived to what God wrote.

The greatest tragedy in the modern Church is not failure  - it is misidentification. Men and women fill pews, function in false roles, and suffocate in the garments of borrowed expectations. They have put on Saul's armor when God called them to sling stones like David. They've settled into the herd when they were destined to lead the charge.

But you  - you feel the stir. Deep down, a frustration grows. The life you've been living no longer fits. The old man is tight. It itches. It offends your spirit. That discomfort is not rebellion  - it is revelation. The Spirit of God is summoning you into metamorphosis. *"Put off the old man… be renewed in the spirit of your mind… and put on the new man, created according to God in true righteousness and holiness"* (Ephesians 4:22-24). It's time to transition. It's time to put on the man you were always meant to be.

1

Like David, your journey is not linear. You may have been a shepherd, a singer, a soldier, or even a misfit - but all those roles were preparation. David's true calling wasn't any of those things. It was kingship. And until you walk in what you were born to rule, everything else will feel like exile.

"To be misidentified is to be disqualified." You will never hear "Well done" if you were merely faithful to a task. You must be faithful to your design. This is the difference between the servant who multiplied his talent and the one who buried it. The fearful man was not just lazy - he was afraid to become who God called him to be (Matthew 25:24-26).

This book is your call to war - not against people, but against average, against cloning, against religious assumption and the spirit of the herd. *Who has believed our report? And to whom has the arm of the Lord been revealed?"* (Isaiah 53:1). The herd will never understand the voice that calls you out. The masses will never celebrate your emergence - until it's undeniable. But you were never called to echo. You were called to roar.

This is your moment of Holy confrontation. The treasure is in your earthen vessel (2 Corinthians 4:7). The question is not whether you have it - the question is whether you'll dig it out. You were called to throw further than others - to operate in hyperbolē - the excellence of power that comes from God alone.

So lift your hands and pray the dangerous prayer:

"Holy Spirit, redefine me. Show me to me."

This is not a motivational book. It is a spiritual excavation. It is a prophetic unlocking. If you're satisfied being faithful but fruitless, close these pages now. But if something in you is crying, "This is not the end - I was made for more!", then turn the page.

Your journey into the Unique Factor

# Chapter One

## The Tragedy of Living Undiscovered

### Biblical Introduction: A Cry from Heaven

There is a cry echoing from the throne of Heaven - not of anger, but of anguish. It is the cry of a Father whose children have forgotten who they are. This divine lament is not over sin alone, but over misidentification. The greatest tragedy in the Church is not rebellion - it is undiscovery. *"My people are destroyed for lack of knowledge"* (Hosea 4:6). Not knowledge of theology. Not knowledge of rituals. But knowledge of identity. Before you were formed in the womb, Heaven wrote your name in a book (Jeremiah 1:5; Psalm 40:7; Hebrews 10:7). That book exists. And one day, your life will be measured against its pages. The question will not be, "Did you survive?" It will be, "Did you become who I designed you to be?"

### A Form of Death Worse Than Dying

Every single person was designed by God for purpose. The worst thing - worse than dying - is not living the life you were born to live. It is a form of death. It is literally a form of death. In your life, Christ decided to do something with you. The moment

5

you get born again, especially, it accelerates. But even before you get born again, God had a design. Whether you're in the Kingdom or not in the Kingdom, there is a design God has for you.

Now, every real message from God - every prophetic message - is usually the result of God revealing the discovery of something within the speaker. This is not something that was learned in a book. This is something God opened in the book of your life while you're having your own discovery.

Living disconnected from that discovery is a slow decay. It's the kind of death where breath still fills your lungs, but purpose has long since exited the room. Many walk the earth dressed in activity but buried in identity. They are the walking dead - functioning, contributing, attending - but not alive. Because until you live what Heaven wrote, everything else is borrowed existence.

You were not designed to wear another man's armor or echo another voice. To live undiscovered is to remain wrapped in the grave clothes of other people's expectations. Jesus called Lazarus forth, but Lazarus wasn't free until He commanded, *"Loose him and let him go"* (John 11:44). Likewise, many believers are resurrected in salvation but still restricted by a lack of revelation. They have been raised, but not released.

The greatest spiritual attack is not against demons - it's against false identity. When you live in a role that God never authored, you become spiritually suffocated. Your potential dies,

6

not because of opposition, but because of omission. The tragedy of the undiscovered life is not that it ends - it's that it never truly begins.

## The 80% Statistic and Occupational Misery

Most people don't hate work - they hate misalignment. Upwards of 80% of the workforce is disengaged, not because they lack talent, but because they lack purpose. They are living under the pressure of performance without the oxygen of assignment. They clock in, grind through routines, perform well, and go home depleted. They are living the wrong life skillfully.

This is the agony of misplaced design - functioning without fulfillment. They are "able to do the job but unable to rejoice in it." Why? Because the job was never theirs to begin with. They are caught in the machinery of expectation, where purpose has been replaced by productivity. They were built for word but sold into labor. They earn a paycheck but hemorrhage passion. They wear suits, carry titles, and lead meetings - yet internally, they are wandering.

The workplace becomes a prison when it isn't aligned with your purpose. "What you do must come out of who you are. If not, you'll succeed in things Heaven never assigned." It's not about your degree. It's about your design. Education without alignment is misdirection. To live misaligned is to have your soul on mute. Every day becomes a burden instead of a broadcast.

Your calling is not a career - it is the unveiling of your divine fingerprint.

God never intended for your labor to be divorced from your identity. Your job should be an altar, not a dungeon. If you're not worshipping through your work, you're not working in your lane. Misplacement produces misery, no matter the salary. Until you locate your divine function, the fruit will never satisfy.

## Calling vs. Competence

Competence can make you useful, but calling makes you dangerous. Competence may get you a platform, but only calling will sustain your soul. There are many people performing roles they mastered through discipline but never received through revelation. They are effective, but empty. They know the script, but they've lost their sound. They look successful, but Heaven knows the truth.

You can be skilled at a task and still starve spiritually. You can be applauded by people and unnoticed by Heaven. Calling is not about doing what you're good at - it's about doing what you were born for. *"The gifts and calling of God are without repentance"* (Romans 11:29), but that doesn't mean they operate in alignment. It's possible for your gift to function while your soul malfunctions.

Competence is teachable. Calling is discoverable. One comes through mentorship; the other through revelation. You can learn technique, but you must unearth nature. Your divine design is not improved by education - it is revealed through encounter.

Calling is about congruence with Heaven. Saul was competent to wear the crown, but he lacked the internal nature of kingship. He ruled from insecurity, while David ruled from identity. That's why David didn't fight Goliath in Saul's armor. He knew - what doesn't fit will not flow. You cannot fight spiritual giants wearing the garments of imitation.

When you discover your nature, authority becomes instinctive. You stop asking for permission to be what God has already called you. True calling is like breathing - natural, rhythmic, essential. It flows out of who you are, not just what you know. And until you walk in that truth, competence will always compete with your calling.

## Prophetic Messages Are Born from Personal Discovery

Prophetic messages are not speeches - they are surgical strikes. They are not merely spoken - they are embodied. They don't originate from intellect but from encounter. The truest prophetic utterance comes when a man has discovered himself in the presence of God. Revelation is not always learned - it is often burned into the soul by the fires of transformation.

Before Jeremiah spoke to nations, he heard Heaven speak to him: *"Before I formed you in the womb, I knew you"* (Jeremiah 1:5). Identity precedes assignment. You cannot carry a word for others until you've received a word about yourself. Self-discovery is not selfish - it is prophetic preparation. When God opens your book, the message isn't secondhand - it's branded by authenticity.

Real prophetic messages don't echo - they erupt. They don't mimic - they manifest. They're born out of fire, not flattery. The man who has met God in the mirror is far more dangerous than the man who has mastered theology. Heaven doesn't just anoint research - it anoints revelation forged in the crucible of identity.

You can't release what you haven't realized. Prophetic clarity increases with personal congruence. When who you are aligns with what you say, authority flows. The weight of your words will never exceed the weight of your walk. You carry force when you carry yourself in the truth of who you are.

This is why self-discovery is not optional. It is the womb of prophetic fire. You don't find your voice in someone else's revelation. You find it in your own excavation. The more you uncover your divine nature, the more potent your message becomes. When you speak from the scroll God wrote about you, your words carry voltage that shakes atmospheres.

## The Cost of Unlived Purpose

There is a cost to ignoring what God wrote. It is not just personal disappointment - it is cosmic delay. Every purpose left dormant is a divine solution unreleased. Heaven doesn't judge effort; it judges alignment. The servant who buried his talent wasn't punished for rebellion - he was judged for inactivity. *"I was afraid and hid your talent in the ground"* (Matthew 25:25). That fear masked itself as caution, but Heaven named it negligence.

The tragedy of the undiscovered is not just in what they lose, but in what others miss. Unlived purpose starves the world of breakthrough. It leaves prayers unanswered and destinies deferred. Your disobedience doesn't die with you - it echoes into generations.

Many have been trained to equate safety with wisdom. But in the Kingdom, faith looks like risk. Obedience often sounds like insanity to the carnal mind. Yet God doesn't measure your life by how well you avoided pain - He measures it by how deeply you fulfilled your scroll.

You don't get to invent your purpose - you discover it. And what you fail to discover, you cannot steward. Heaven has no rewards for the man who played it safe. The crowns are reserved for those who bled in obedience. Those who laid their ambitions on the altar of assignment.

The cost of unlived purpose is generational silence. Songs that will never be sung. Books that will never be written. Movements that will never be born. Because someone chose comfort over calling. Someone chose survival over surrender.

And this is why the cry of Heaven echoes: *"Where are you?"* (Genesis 3:9). Not as a geographical inquiry - but as a spiritual confrontation. The question is a summons. It's not about your position on the map - it's about your posture in destiny.

To live undiscovered is to delay the Kingdom. It is to walk through life like a sealed scroll, never read, never opened, never poured out. But if you dare to respond to the divine question, if you choose to answer the call of your original design, the silence ends and the story begins.

## The Awakening of Identity Begins with a Question

"Adam, where are you?" These are not the words of a confused deity - they are the words of a Father initiating divine confrontation. God knew where Adam was geographically. What He was asking was far deeper: Where are you in identity? In alignment? In purpose?

Heaven's questions are not for God's benefit - they are for yours. The question is designed to awaken, to provoke, to confront. Adam had lost more than location - he had lost himself. The echo of that question still reverberates through every generation: Where are you?

Until you locate yourself in the Spirit, you cannot step into your scroll. You cannot repent for where you are if you do not recognize how far you've drifted. The prodigal son didn't return because of a sermon - he returned because "he came to himself." The mirror moment came before the miracle.

When Heaven asks a question, it's not seeking data - it's issuing a summons. Divine questions uncover assumptions, strip away illusions, and demand honesty. Where are you? Not your ministry title. Not your income. Not your reputation. Where are you in relation to who God designed you to be?

You cannot fake your way into discovery. The only path forward is brutal clarity. The Spirit of God is still asking, *"Where are you?"* - not because He lost you, but because you lost you. Identity begins to reawaken the moment you stop pretending and start repenting.

This is the sacred intersection of recognition and response. The moment where pretending dies and purpose is resurrected. You must pray the dangerous prayer: "Holy Spirit, show me to me." Until you are exposed, you cannot be equipped. Until you are honest, you cannot be healed.

Prophetic transformation always begins with a question. That question is your invitation. Your confrontation. Your deliverance. Answer it - and you step into divine discovery.

## Conclusion: The Dangerous Prayer of Discovery

You are not permitted to die a stranger to your design. You were never meant to blend in with the herd or mimic someone else's calling. You are not an echo - you are a voice. And Heaven is waiting for that voice to rise.

13

The undiscovered life is not a season - it is a deception. You cannot walk in power while living in disguise. There must be a divine unveiling. The scroll of your life cannot be read until the seal of fear is broken. Your alignment is overdue. Your emergence is necessary. The Kingdom cannot afford another mute warrior.

You must pray the dangerous prayer: "Holy Spirit, show me to me." That prayer will shake foundations. It will shatter false layers and resurrect buried design. You were never called to conform. You were born to confront - to confront every lie, every label, every limitation that Hell tried to impose on your nature.

The world does not need another performer. It needs prophets forged in the fire of identity. You are not here to survive. You are here to awaken. And when you step into your true name, everything changes. Atmospheres shift. Chains break. Generations pivot.

This is your moment. Not to strive - but to surrender. Not to hustle - but to align. Not to pretend - but to discover. You are the scroll. You are the voice. You are the evidence that God is still writing destinies.

So rise. And be discovered.

**Scripture Index**

- Hosea 4:6
- Jeremiah 1:5
- Psalm 40:7-8
- Hebrews 10:7

- John 11:44
- John 10:10
- Romans 11:29
- Matthew 25:25
- Genesis 3:9
- 2 Corinthians 4:7

# Chapter Two

## You Were Created with Original Design

There was nothing accidental about your formation. You were not mass-produced. You were meticulously crafted by the breath and intention of God. You were born in the mind of God long before you were born in your mother's womb. You are not the product of a random sequence of events - you are the fulfillment of divine intention. Everything about you was written in His scroll. Your personality, your giftings, your inclinations, your burdens - all of it points back to a specific design meant to reflect the nature of your Creator and reveal the purpose of your existence.

### Design Was the First Act of Love

Before there was sin, before there was shame, there was design. And that design was not driven by function alone but by affection. God didn't make you because He had to - He made you because He wanted to. You are the result of Heaven's desire. The scripture says, *"Before I formed you in the womb, I knew you"* (Jeremiah 1:5). You were known. You were desired. You were sent.

When you realize that design came before dysfunction, everything changes. You stop living to fix what's wrong with you and begin awakening to what's right with you. You stop chasing affirmation and start walking in alignment. The blueprint is not hidden - it's waiting. Heaven isn't confused about who you are. Only Babylon is.

Design is the signature of love. Before you had a body, you had a blueprint. Before you were wounded, you were wanted. Before the world tried to define you, Heaven already did. That's why no amount of rejection from people can nullify the acceptance of your Maker. You were not an afterthought. You were His first thought. *"I praise you, for I am fearfully and wonderfully made. Wonderful are your works; my soul knows it very well"* (Psalm 139:14).

## The Power of Intentionality

God does nothing randomly. Every detail of your makeup was chosen with purpose. He didn't give you your temperament so you could tame it - He gave it so you could channel it. He didn't place desires in your heart to torment you - He placed them as clues to your calling. *"We are God's workmanship, created in Christ Jesus for good works, which God prepared beforehand"* (Ephesians 2:10). Your design is not accidental - it's prophetic.

Everything in you is intentional. Every urge, every burden, every Holy frustration - it's Heaven speaking in the language of design. You do not have to seek your assignment outside of yourself when God hid it within. You are carrying Kingdom technology beneath your skin. The more you understand your design, the less you chase affirmation from broken systems.

The reason some things bother you that don't bother others is because your spirit is coded to respond. That's intentional. That's design. Your wiring isn't wrong. It's sacred. Stop trying to edit what Heaven authored. *"The plans of the heart belong to man, but the answer of the tongue is from the Lord"* (Proverbs 16:1).

## Distinction Is Not Dysfunction

The enemy wants to convince you that what makes you different is a defect. But Heaven calls it distinction. You were never meant to blend in. You are salt. You are light. You are a city on a hill that cannot be hidden (Matthew 5:14). What they called "too much" was actually your anointing in disguise. What they labeled as odd, God called original.

You were not sent to echo the crowd - you were sent to confront it. Every time you tried to shrink, it was a war against your own design. You cannot be free until you love what God loved when He made you. When you embrace your design, you no longer chase acceptance - you release authority.

Being misunderstood is the tax of distinction. You were not built to fit rooms - you were built to change them. Your uniqueness is a weapon. The moment you embrace your peculiarity is the moment you become dangerous to mediocrity.

God's remnant is never generic. It's always prophetic. You're not broken - you're branded. *"But you are a chosen people, a royal priesthood, a Holy nation, God's special possession..."* (1 Peter 2:9).

## Your Nature Is Your Navigation

You don't have to search for purpose in the world when purpose is wired into your being. The clues are in your cravings. What makes you righteously angry? What causes your heart to break? What brings tears without warning? These are indicators of your divine compass. *"Delight yourself in the Lord, and He will give you the desires of your heart"* (Psalm 37:4). That doesn't mean He grants your wish list - it means He plants the right desires.

Many wander through life searching for a voice from Heaven when they've been ignoring the voice within. God does not just speak externally - He leads internally. Your design was built to respond to divine direction. But until you honor your wiring, you'll mistake discomfort for disobedience and ignore what was meant to direct you.

You don't need a prophetic word to know your purpose. Your nature is already pointing toward it. What moves you, burdens you, and calls you in the quiet places - those are divine signals. Follow them. Your tears are often more prophetic than your sermons. Your broken heart is the map to your breakthrough. *"It is God who works in you to will and to act in order to fulfill his good purpose"* (Philippians 2:13).

## Originality Demands Separation

To walk in your design means to walk away from every environment that mocks it. You cannot become who you were meant to be while staying where everyone expects you to conform. Abraham had to leave his father's house to receive his true inheritance (Genesis 12:1). Separation is not punishment - it's permission.

Your original design is suffocated in atmospheres of imitation. You were not called to maintain culture - you were called to recreate it. And that kind of calling will always be too loud for controlled rooms. When God begins to reveal your design, you'll find yourself misunderstood, mislabeled, and misquoted. Don't shrink. Stay loud. Stay aligned.

The crowd will always try to domesticate your difference. But you cannot carry reformation and be obsessed with reputation. The wilderness is where originals are forged. It's where noise is stripped and the scroll is revealed. And only when you dare to be separate will Heaven dare to release the fullness of your call. *"Do not be conformed to this world, but be transformed by the renewing of your mind…"* (Romans 12:2).

## Agreement Unlocks Assignment

Heaven can only fund what you agree with. As long as you reject your design, you'll block your provision. God doesn't anoint potential - He anoints alignment. Until you say yes to who you are, you are living beneath your anointing. *"Can two walk together unless they are agreed?"* (Amos 3:3).

Agreement isn't just about doctrine - it's about identity. You can't walk in power while warring with your design. When you finally stop apologizing for who you are, the resources of Heaven will begin to back your every move. What felt blocked will flow. What was stuck will move. Because you finally stepped into the frequency of Heaven's original intent.

Heaven waits for your yes. Not a yes to ministry. A yes to identity. Because you cannot fulfill your assignment while rejecting your authenticity. Hell's greatest weapon isn't sin - it's self-rejection. When you agree with your design, you disarm the lies that tried to bind you. *"The steps of a righteous man are ordered by the Lord"* (Psalm 37:23).

## Design Is the First Door to Destiny

Destiny doesn't begin with a stage - it begins with a mirror. Until you see what God sees, you'll chase what He never gave. You were never created to strive for worth - you were born from worth. *"You are fearfully and wonderfully made"* (Psalm 139:14). That is not a poetic line - it is a divine decree.

When you reclaim your design, you reclaim your direction. You stop wandering and start building. You stop comparing and start pioneering. Your voice returns. Your clarity returns. Your joy returns. Because the person God created finally shows up. And the moment you stand in your true identity, everything around you has to adjust.

Design is the permission slip for dominion. You cannot steward the earth while hating your frame. Heaven's blueprint is not optional - it's essential. You don't start with calling - you start with clarity. And when you see yourself rightly, you stop asking for open doors and start building them. *"For we live by faith, not by sight"* (2 Corinthians 5:7).

## Conclusion: Return to the Blueprint

The original you is not missing. He's just been buried under years of comparison, fear, and performance. But Heaven is issuing a summons: come out. Return to the blueprint. Shake off the residue of Babylon. Peel off the layers of false identity. And dare to believe that you were enough before the world tried to edit you.

Say it: I agree with Heaven. I accept my design. I return to my scroll.

## Scripture Index:

- Jeremiah 1:5
- Ephesians 2:10
- Matthew 5:14
- Psalm 37:4
- Genesis 12:1
- Amos 3:3
- Psalm 139:14
- Proverbs 16:1

- 1 Peter 2:9
- Philippians 2:13
- Romans 12:2

- Psalm 37:23
- 2 Corinthians 5:7

# Chapter Three

## The Power of Prophetic Discovery

### Biblical Introduction: When God Asks Questions

From the beginning of time, the voice of God didn't just speak answers - He asked questions. Not because He lacked knowledge, but because He desired revelation. In the garden, after Adam fell, God called, *"Where are you?"* (Genesis 3:9). It wasn't curiosity. It was confrontation. A divine interrogation meant to provoke self-awareness. In that moment, Heaven introduced a truth that still reverberates through every generation: sometimes the most prophetic thing God can give you is a question.

This chapter unveils the power of prophetic discovery - the moments when God doesn't just tell you who you are, but prompts you to uncover it. Revelation isn't always lightning; sometimes it's a mirror. God will ask you what you want, who you are, and why you're here. Not to embarrass, but to expose. Not to shame, but to summon. Because until you answer Heaven's questions, you will remain hidden beneath assumptions and wrapped in roles He never wrote. This is the hour to awaken. To stop living off borrowed insight. To discover the power of your prophetic identity.

## The Prophet's Role: Clarifying Calling and Identity

The role of the prophet has never been to entertain curiosity - it is to provoke clarity. Prophetic voices don't simply predict the future; they call out your blueprint. They point to what has been written in Heaven's scrolls about you (Psalm 139:16; Hebrews 10:7; Revelation 10:8-11). When a true prophetic voice enters your life, confusion is confronted. It doesn't answer every question - it awakens the right ones.

A real prophet reveals not what looks impressive, but what Heaven authored. They speak into your original design, not your religious costume. They confront false assignments, burn up man-made aspirations, and ignite Heaven's purpose. Their voice becomes a chisel to sculpt your soul back into divine shape. They do not affirm the version of you that pleases the crowd. They call forth the version that terrifies Hell.

Prophetic insight does not replace discovery - it initiates it. The danger is when people idolize prophets, thinking they will receive an exact map for their life. But God doesn't outsource discovery. He partners with it. Even if someone calls out your calling, you must still uncover it. You must steward the revelation through obedience. Because prophecy is never meant to relieve you of responsibility.

Prophecy reveals potential, but it does not force obedience. It announces the scroll, but you must turn the pages. You are accountable for what you hear. Paul told Timothy to "wage war" with the prophecies made about him (1 Timothy 1:18). That means every word from Heaven must be fought for, contended with, and walked out.

You can't walk in your scroll with someone else's shoes. Every word must lead you to the Word Himself. Every prophecy must push you toward intimacy. Otherwise, you are just collecting declarations while ignoring direction.

## The Encounter with the Pastor's Daughter

In a church service packed with expectancy and praise, a young woman approached with a question wrapped in assumption: "Can you tell me what I'm supposed to do with my life?" The room paused, and the air tensed. She assumed a prophet could shortcut her journey. But Heaven doesn't trade destiny for ease. The prophet replied, "What do you want to do?"

It was not a deflection. It was a divine setup. Because sometimes you don't need a prophecy - you need a question. Questions force introspection. They call forth dormant identity. God never asked Adam, "Where are you?" to gain information - He asked so Adam could recognize his own dislocation. In that moment, the young woman realized: clarity doesn't come from outsourcing your future to a prophet. It comes from discovering your nature.

Many people are waiting for confirmation about a calling they haven't even bothered to investigate. They want clarity without intimacy, direction without dialogue. But you cannot build your life on borrowed prophecy. If you live off another man's revelation, you will never walk in your own authority.

Jesus asked blind Bartimaeus, *"What do you want Me to do for you?"* (Mark 10:51). It was obvious the man was blind. But the question was for him, not for Jesus. It was a call to clarity. A confrontation of desire. The same way God challenged Elijah's cave with, *"What are you doing here?"* (1 Kings 19:9). Destiny begins with a question.

## Insight Without Revelation Is Insufficient

Spiritual insight is not the same as spiritual revelation. Insight is seeing a thing. Revelation is becoming it. You can perceive truth without embodying it. You can know what you should do and still not do it. *"We know in part and we prophesy in part"* (1 Corinthians 13:9). But partial sight is dangerous if it creates full dependency.

Prophetic discovery requires that you move beyond inspiration into incarnation. You can't just admire the word - you must become the word. Jesus didn't just preach the Kingdom; He embodied it. And until the prophetic word becomes flesh in you, it remains potential, not power.

God is not interested in you quoting destiny while living dislocated. There is a difference between hearing who you are and discovering who you are. And the difference is obedience. Revelation becomes reality when you walk it out.

James writes, *"Be doers of the word, and not hearers only, deceiving yourselves"* (James 1:22). You can be full of insight and still empty of transformation. Hearing the voice of God is not the goal. Becoming the echo of that voice is.

## Why Questions Can Be More Prophetic Than Answers

When God wants to transform you, He often begins with a question. *"What do you see, Jeremiah?"* (Jeremiah 1:11). *"Can these bones live?"* (Ezekiel 37:3). *"Who do you say I am?"* (Matthew 16:15). These questions were not for God's benefit - they were invitations into encounter. Questions expose your perspective. They reveal your readiness.

God asked Adam, "Where are you?" not because He didn't know - but because Adam didn't. The original Hebrew carries the idea: "How did you get here?" That question still reverberates. How did you get here? Why are you still stuck in a job you hate? Why are you functioning outside your nature?

A prophetic question can shake you free from cycles. It can deliver you from borrowed identity. When God begins to question you, it is not condemnation - it is confrontation. He is not trying to embarrass you. He is trying to awaken you. Because you cannot change what you will not name.

God asked Elijah, *"What are you doing here?"* (1 Kings 19:9).
Not because He didn't know Elijah's physical location, but
because Elijah had fled from identity. Heaven asks dangerous
questions to deliver us from safe assumptions.

## Discovering Nature Before Education

Before you educate your mind, you must discover your
nature. This is the reversal of the world's system. The world says,
"Get the degree, then choose your path." The Kingdom says,
"Discover your design, then educate that design."

There are countless stories of people with advanced
degrees working in unrelated fields, dissatisfied and disconnected.
Why? Because information without identity is futility. It doesn't
matter what you're trained to do if it isn't who you were born to
be.

Your nature is the fingerprint of God on your soul. It is the
part of you that flows without effort, burns without burnout, and
thrives without applause. When you discover your nature,
everything else begins to align. Education becomes confirmation,
not compensation.

Romans 12:6 reminds us, *"We have different gifts, according to
the grace given to each of us."* Your education must match your grace.
Otherwise, it becomes a burden, not a blessing. Paul said, *"By the
grace of God I am what I am"* (1 Corinthians 15:10). Your grace
reveals your lane. Your nature reveals your grace.

29

You are not what you were taught - you are what you were designed to be. Your gifts are not electives. They are essential. And if you don't educate your nature, you will spend your life performing roles you were never built to sustain.

## Your Dream Life Is About to Explode

Dreams are not random. They are divine previews. They are Heaven's language to the subconscious. And when you begin the journey of prophetic discovery, your dream life shifts. It intensifies. It multiplies. Because your spirit begins to align with your scroll.

Dreams are often ignored because people don't recognize their prophetic nature. But Scripture is clear: God speaks in dreams (Job 33:14-16). Your night visions are not leftovers of the day's stress - they are spiritual downloads waiting to be interpreted.

Joseph's life was shaped by dreams (Genesis 37:5-11). Daniel received a national strategy through dreams and interpretations (Daniel 2:19). Pilate's wife warned him of Jesus' innocence because of a dream (Matthew 27:19). Dreams are not to be dismissed. They are often prophetic instructions.

When you begin to pursue who you were designed to be, Heaven responds with increased spiritual communication. You will begin to dream more. See more. Hear more. Not because you're special - but because you're finally aligned.

The prophetic isn't reserved for the elite. It's awakened in the hungry. And when you dare to ask the right questions, when you confront the comfortable, when you cry out for clarity, Heaven will flood your sleep with revelation.

Raise your hands and declare: "Holy Spirit, show me to me. Show me who You made me to be. Interrupt my sleep. Invade my day. Speak until I am awakened."

## Conclusion: Stop Looking for a Map. Become the Movement.

You are not called to follow a formula. You are called to follow a voice. Prophetic discovery is not a one-time moment - it is a lifestyle of pursuit. Stop asking for directions from people who never left the parking lot. Stop waiting for others to validate what God already confirmed.

You are not waiting on another word. You are being called to walk in the ones you already received. And if you will dare to walk, to ask, to dream, to obey - the veil will lift. The scroll will open. The dormant parts of you will roar to life.

You don't need to be told what to do next. You need to become who God said you are.

Because in becoming, everything else becomes clear.

## Scripture Index:

- Genesis 3:9
- Psalm 139:16

- Hebrews 10:7
- Revelation 10:8-11
- 1 Timothy 1:18
- Mark 10:51
- 1 Kings 19:9
- 1 Corinthians 13:9
- James 1:22
- Jeremiah 1:11
- Ezekiel 37:3
- Matthew 16:15
- Romans 12:6
- 1 Corinthians 15:10
- Job 33:14-16
- Genesis 37:5-11
- Daniel 2:19
- Matthew 27:19

# Chapter Four

## Discover Your Nature, Educate Your Nature

**Biblical Introduction:**

**From Heaven's Blueprint to Earth's Assignment**

Before you ever picked up a pencil, God had already written your scroll. Before you ever applied to a school, He had already assigned your territory. Heaven never intended for you to be shaped by the world's system before discovering your divine nature. "Before I formed you in the womb, I knew you; before you were born, I sanctified you" (Jeremiah 1:5). Identity precedes education. Calling comes before credentials. Revelation must lead before instruction can take root. This chapter is not a suggestion - it's a divine confrontation. Discover who you are before you try to become something else.

### The Power of Authenticity in Vocation

Heaven doesn't fund clones. God doesn't anoint copies. The Kingdom moves through authenticity, not mimicry. The world applauds adaptation; Heaven demands authenticity. Until you discover who you are, you will educate what you are not.

You were never called to fit a mold. You were called to be the mold breaker. Authenticity is not personality - it's prophetic nature. The anointing does not rest on imitation. It flows where identity is honored. *"We have different gifts, according to the grace given to each of us"* (Romans 12:6).

Jesus never called His disciples to mimic one another. He didn't say, "Be like Peter," or "Echo John." He said, *"Follow Me"* (Matthew 4:19). The call is to follow the voice, not the pattern. When God calls you, He calls the real you - not the rehearsed one.

The Church was never meant to be a factory of duplicates. It was designed to be a house of originals. Apostles don't duplicate ministries - they activate mantles. Prophets don't create clones - they awaken uniqueness. Heaven's creativity is not confined to trends. It flows through truth. Truth of identity. Truth of assignment. Truth of purpose.

Paul wrote, *"By the grace of God I am what I am"* (1 Corinthians 15:10). He didn't apologize for his difference - he stewarded it. You are not meant to suppress your divine distinction to fit religious norms. You are called to walk in it with fire.

When your assignment matches your authenticity, grace multiplies. Joy deepens. Effectiveness explodes. But when you build a career in conflict with your design, frustration becomes your reward. *"A man's gift makes room for him and brings him before great men"* (Proverbs 18:16). Not his mimicry - his gift.

**Statistics on Degree Irrelevance**

The world is filled with miseducated people. Degrees without direction. Diplomas earned in ignorance of design. It is no wonder that 80% of college graduates never work in their field. They followed advice without discovering their nature. They learned a trade that had no covenant with their calling.

The world taught them how to learn - but not who they are. It handed them tests, not truth. Instruction without introspection is malpractice. It is dangerous to develop skill apart from self-awareness. *"The heart of the discerning acquires knowledge, for the ears of the wise seek it out"* (Proverbs 18:15).

People sit in classrooms learning formulas but never discovering fire. They earn letters behind their name while their soul shrivels in silence. Why? Because they educated their bios (biological/natural life) while neglecting their Zoe (spiritual life, the kind of life that Jesus lived). They chased certification while ignoring calling.

Many spend years and thousands of dollars educating a version of themselves that God never authored. They become professionals in professions they hate, all while their true calling gathers dust. They do not fail because they lacked opportunity. They fail because they lacked discovery. *"There is a way that seems right to a man, but its end is the way to death"* (Proverbs 14:12).

This is why Paul warned in Romans 12:2, *"Do not conform to the pattern of this world, but be transformed by the renewing of your mind."* Conformity educates copies. Revelation transforms sons.

## Discovering Nature Through Repetition

The key to discovering your divine nature is repetition. What do you do instinctively? What do you repeat with ease, joy, and precision? Your nature is not buried in mystery - it is hidden in consistency. God doesn't hide your purpose from you. He hides it in you. And it keeps trying to come out.

David didn't become a giant killer because he trained for war. He became one because he repeated worship. He mastered the sling while watching sheep (1 Samuel 17:34-36). What you repeat in private becomes your weapon in public. *"Whatever your hand finds to do, do it with all your might"* (Ecclesiastes 9:10).

Jesus Himself repeated the pattern of retreating to pray (Luke 5:16). He didn't stumble into power - He stewarded it through repetition. Even His miracles flowed from a rhythm of presence. Your patterns prophesy. What you do repeatedly reveals who you were always meant to be.

Ask yourself: What do I do naturally that others consider supernatural? What comes out of me effortlessly that blesses others deeply? Repetition is not redundancy - it is revelation. It reveals grace. It unveils flow.

Track your joy. Follow your flow. And you will find your fingerprint.

## False Dreams and Misapplied Ambition

You can educate a lie. You can anoint an illusion. Many are chasing dreams that are not divine - they are desperate reactions to rejection. Their goals were not born from vision but from vengeance. They want to prove something rather than fulfill something.

You must discern the difference between God's dream and your defense mechanism. Just because you're good at something doesn't mean you're graced for it. The enemy doesn't need you to sin - he just needs you to succeed at the wrong thing.

Cain offered an acceptable sacrifice to himself but not to God (Genesis 4:3-5). His ambition was religious but misaligned. And it led to murder. The danger of misapplied ambition is that it looks spiritual while creating death.

Ambition without authenticity is dangerous. It leads to burnout, bitterness, and spiritual bankruptcy. Jesus said, *"I do nothing on my own but speak just what the Father has taught me"* (John 8:28). He didn't move out of pressure. He moved out of permission. *"Unless the Lord builds the house, the builders labor in vain"* (Psalm 127:1).

Ask yourself: What dream have I adopted that doesn't match my design? What ambition have I spiritualized that God never sanctified? You cannot run from rejection into your assignment. You must be called into it.

## Talent vs. Assignment: Know the Difference

Talent is what you can do. Assignment is what you must do. Talent is optional. Assignment is eternal. There are many things you are good at, but only one thing you are anointed for. Do not confuse ability with authority.

You can have talent that draws a crowd, and still be far from your calling. Saul looked like a king but didn't carry the oil. David was a shepherd, but the oil knew his name (1 Samuel 16:1-13). It is not about what you do well. It's about what you were made for. *"Many are called, but few are chosen"* (Matthew 22:14).

Jesus had the talent to lead armies, but He chose the cross. Paul had the education to climb religious ranks, but he chose prison and purpose. Your calling is not about ease - it's about impact. Paul writes in Ephesians 2:10, *"For we are God's handiwork, created in Christ Jesus to do good works, which God prepared in advance for us to do."*

Your assignment is not what excites people - it's what awakens you. It is the thing that fuels you when applause is absent. It carries weight, but it also carries joy. It may cost you everything, but it will produce eternal fruit. *"I press on to take hold of that for which Christ Jesus took hold of me"* (Philippians 3:12).

## Nature Is the Blueprint for Worship

Worship is not a genre. It is not a song. Worship is alignment with design. When you live in your nature, you worship.

When you function as God created you, you release fragrance to Heaven.

Romans 12:1 says, *"Offer your bodies as a living sacrifice, Holy and pleasing to God - this is your true and proper worship."* That means worship is not a moment - it's a manifestation. It's not about singing louder - it's about living truer.

Abel brought the right offering because he understood his nature. Cain brought what was convenient. One triggered favor. The other triggered wrath. Worship without identity is noise. Worship with identity is fire.

Hebrews 11:4 says, *"By faith Abel brought God a better offering than Cain did. By faith he was commended as righteous."* Faith is not just belief - it's alignment. When you act in sync with who God made you to be, Heaven answers with glory.

Worship begins where identity is honored. Until you align with your divine wiring, you're just performing. But once you operate from identity, everything becomes worship - your work, your creativity, your leadership, your speech. Heaven responds not to talent, but to truth.

## Living from Zoe Life, Not Bios Life

There are two types of life in Scripture: Bios and Zoe. Bios is natural life - your schedule, your breath, your biology. Zoe is divine life - the Spirit-fueled essence that flows from God Himself. Many believers are existing on bios while starving for Zoe.

Jesus said, *"I have come that they may have life* (Zoe), *and have it to the full"* (John 10:10). Zoe is not survival - it's overflow. It's not routine - it's revelation. It's not busy - it's burning with divine energy.

Paul reminds us, *"For to me, to live is Christ and to die is gain"* (Philippians 1:21). That is Zoe talking. It's not just existence - it's embodiment. When you live from Zoe, your work becomes worship, your purpose becomes propulsion, and your nature becomes fuel. You no longer chase identity - you radiate it.

Titus 3:5 reminds us, *"He saved us through the washing of rebirth and renewal by the Holy Spirit."* Zoe life is Spirit life. It doesn't operate on effort but overflow. It doesn't burn out - it burns bright.

Bios life looks stable but feels dry. Zoe life looks risky but feels alive. If you're bored, bitter, or burned out - you're not living from Zoe. You're surviving off bios. It's time to switch systems. It's time to reconnect with the divine current that created you.

## Scripture Index:

- John 8:28
- Psalm 127:1
- 1 Samuel 16:1-13
- Matthew 22:14
- Ephesians 2:10
- Philippians 3:12

- Romans 12:1
- Hebrews 11:4
- John 10:10
- Philippians 1:21
- Titus 3:5

# Chapter Five

## Put on the New Man

You were never called to improve the old man. You were summoned to bury him. There is no anointing to upgrade what God sentenced to die. The cross was not a cosmetic fix - it was an execution site. The Kingdom does not reform the flesh. It crucifies it. And from that grave of former identity rises a new man - clothed in Christ, governed by Spirit, driven by divine design.

### The Grave of the Old Man

Every transformation begins with a funeral. The cross is not just a historical event; it is a spiritual necessity. It is the dividing line between who you were and who you are becoming. You cannot live resurrected while dragging the corpse of your former self. *"Knowing this, that our old man is crucified with him..."* (Romans 6:6). The cross doesn't ask you to negotiate with your dysfunction - it demands you nail it.

Too many believers are dressing up the old man, trying to make him presentable for church, palatable for ministry, and tolerable for leadership. But Heaven has no tolerance for what was never born of it. The new man doesn't coexist with the old -

he replaces him. You cannot wear a new mantle while clinging to an expired identity. *"If anyone is in Christ, he is a new creation. The old has passed away; behold, the new has come."* (2 Corinthians 5:17).

This burial is not symbolic. It is spiritual law. The old man was not redeemed - he was terminated. Your resurrection life is the evidence that grace didn't come to cohabit with carnality - it came to evict it. *"I have been crucified with Christ. It is no longer I who live, but Christ who lives in me..."* (Galatians 2:20).

## The Wardrobe of the New

The new man is not a feeling. He is a decision. He is not fabricated from your emotions. He is forged by your agreement. *"Put on the new man, which after God is created in righteousness and true holiness"* (Ephesians 4:24). You do not stumble into the new - you step into it. It is not automatic. It is activated by revelation and obedience.

Putting on the new man is not behavior modification - it is identity activation. It is awakening to what already exists in the spirit. You are not becoming someone else - you are shedding who you were never meant to be. The wardrobe of the new is holiness, humility, courage, and clarity. It fits differently because it was tailored in Heaven. *"Do not lie to one another, seeing that you have put off the old self with its practices and have put on the new self..."* (Colossians 3:9-10).

God does not give robes to rebels. The new garment is for those who surrender. And once you put it on, it will not fit your former places. It was never meant to match the environment you were delivered from. *"Let us cast off the works of darkness and put on the armor of light"* (Romans 13:12).

## Identity Is a Garment

Garments in scripture often symbolize identity. Joseph's coat marked him. Elijah's mantle commissioned Elisha. Adam and Eve lost their covering when sin entered. And now, through Christ, we are clothed with power from on high. You are not naked in the spirit - you are robed with revelation. But garments must be put on. *"Clothe yourselves with the Lord Jesus Christ"* (Romans 13:14).

You wear what you believe. If you believe you are rejected, you'll dress in insecurity. If you believe you are chosen, you'll wear confidence like armor. Heaven is offering garments, but Hell is offering counterfeits. You must choose your wardrobe daily. Every morning, you either robe yourself in righteousness or wrap yourself in residue. *"I will greatly rejoice in the Lord; my soul shall exult in my God, for he has clothed me with the garments of salvation…"* (Isaiah 61:10).

There are no neutral garments in the Kingdom. You are always clothed in what you carry. The garment of identity will either draw Heaven's endorsement or Babylon's attention.

44

Choose wisely. *"And to her it was granted to be arrayed in fine linen, clean and bright, for the fine linen is the righteous acts of the saints."* (Revelation 19:8).

## Agreement Is Access

You cannot walk in what you won't agree with. Heaven's resources are tied to Heaven's revelation. The new man is not accessed through striving - it's accessed through surrender. *"How can two walk together except they be agreed?"* (Amos 3:3). If you war against your new nature, you will delay your transformation.

Agreement is more than verbal - it is visible. You can't agree with Heaven in private while dressing like Babylon in public. The new man is not for altars alone - it is for battlefields. If you agree with Heaven, your walk changes, your speech changes, your thinking elevates. The power of God does not flow through conflicted vessels. You must align to ignite. *"Do not be unequally yoked with unbelievers..."* (2 Corinthians 6:14).

You cannot walk in Kingdom power while carrying worldly agreements. Alignment is the door. Agreement is the key. *"Agree with God, and be at peace; thereby good will come to you."* (Job 22:21).

## The Language of the New Man

The old man speaks in survival. The new man speaks in surrender. The old man complains, defends, and justifies. The new man decrees, declares, and obeys. *"Death and life are in the power of the tongue...*" (Proverbs 18:21). The tongue is not just a weapon - it is a wardrobe. It either clothes you in Kingdom or strips you in shame.

Language is proof of identity. When you begin to speak what God has spoken, you are no longer echoing culture - you are releasing Kingdom. You silence the narrative of shame by voicing the truth of your adoption. You cancel the lies of the enemy by confessing the word of your scroll. The new man does not speak from wounds - he speaks from wholeness. *"Let your speech always be gracious, seasoned with salt..."* (Colossians 4:6).

Your tongue reveals your transformation. And Heaven listens. *"The Lord listened and heard... and a book of remembrance was written before Him for those who feared the Lord and esteemed His name"* (Malachi 3:16).

## The Posture of Dominion

The new man is not passive. He is not quiet. He does not blend in. He stands in dominion. *"For if by one man's offense death reigned... much more they which receive abundance of grace and the gift of righteousness shall reign in life by one, Jesus Christ"* (Romans 5:17). To reign is to occupy. To rule is to resist the systems that once ruled you.

The new man doesn't ask for permission - he operates from position. You don't need confirmation when you have commission. You were not born to react to Hell - you were anointed to interrupt it. Dominion is not arrogance. It is alignment. And when you posture yourself in authority, demons recognize it, atmospheres shift, and legacies are rewritten. *"Behold, I have given you authority… over all the power of the enemy…"* (Luke 10:19).

True authority never announces itself - it manifests. Hell doesn't respect titles. It responds to truth.

### Warfare and the New Nature

Putting on the new man doesn't exempt you from warfare - it equips you for it. The enemy does not attack your past. He fears your future. Your new man is a threat to every system of compromise you used to tolerate. *"Therefore take up the whole armor of God, that you may be able to withstand in the evil day…"* (Ephesians 6:13). The armor fits the new man - not the old.

You were not dressed for defense - you were dressed for advancement. You are not retreating. You are reclaiming. And the moment you accept your identity, you become a battlefield of breakthrough. You don't fight for identity - you fight from it. That shift changes everything. Hell fears the believer who knows who they are. *"No weapon formed against you shall prosper…"* (Isaiah 54:17).

This armor is not optional. It is survival. You are not invincible - you are equipped. Stay dressed.

### Renewal Is Daily

The new man is not a one-time wardrobe change. It is a daily decision. *"Be renewed in the spirit of your mind"* (Ephesians 4:23).

The Kingdom is not looking for occasional consistency - it demands continual renewal. You cannot conquer today with yesterday's clarity.

Daily renewal is your covenant to live from revelation, not regression. It's your commitment to rise above the noise and enter the counsel of the King. The world offers distraction. The Spirit offers direction. You choose what you listen to. And what you listen to determines what you put on. *"Do not be conformed to this world, but be transformed by the renewing of your mind..."* (Romans 12:2).

Your mind is the battleground, and transformation is not accidental. It is intentional. It is violent. It is sacred.

Conclusion: Arise, Put on the New Man

This is not the hour to negotiate with your old nature. This is the hour to bury it. To strip off the garments of fear, shame, and compromise - and to clothe yourself with righteousness, power, and boldness. You are not who you were. You are not what they called you. You are what He wrote.

Put on the new man. Walk like it. Speak like it. Reign like it. The world is groaning for sons - not survivors. Heaven is waiting for agreement - not excuses. And your scroll will not manifest until the new man stands up.

**Scripture Index:**

- Romans 6:6
- Ephesians 4:24
- Romans 13:14
- Amos 3:3

- Proverbs 18:21
- Romans 5:17
- Ephesians 6:13
- Ephesians 4:23
- 2 Corinthians 5:17
- Colossians 3:9-10
- Isaiah 61:10
- 2 Corinthians 6:14
- Colossians 4:6
- Luke 10:19
- Isaiah 54:17
- Romans 12:2
- Galatians 2:20
- Romans 13:12
- Revelation 19:8
- Job 22:21
- Malachi 3:16

# Chapter Six

## The Voice of the Spirit

There is a frequency that doesn't originate from earth. It bypasses intellect, transcends reason, and pierces the human soul with divine urgency. It is the Voice of the Spirit - clear, sovereign, relentless. The Spirit of God is not silent. He is speaking, directing, calling, and revealing. But not all ears can hear. Because the Spirit speaks not to entertain, but to commission.

### The Spirit Still Speaks

The Spirit of God has not grown quiet in our generation. It is the hearts of men that have grown dull. He still speaks - not through sensationalism but through alignment. *"He who has ears, let him hear what the Spirit says..."* (Revelation 2:7). His voice is not hidden - it is Holy. It demands stillness. It commands attention.

When you live in constant noise, you train your spirit to ignore divine direction. But the Spirit speaks to those who listen with surrender, not suspicion. This voice doesn't flatter - it convicts. It doesn't validate feelings - it commands obedience. Heaven is not echoing your desire. Heaven is issuing instructions. *"Today, if you hear his voice, do not harden your hearts..."* (Hebrews 3:15).

Every word from the Spirit carries fire and clarity. He doesn't speak to fill the silence - He speaks to reveal divine timing and enforce spiritual alignment. *"He sent out his word and healed them, and delivered them from their destruction"* (Psalm 107:20). *"Man shall not live by bread alone, but by every word that proceeds from the mouth of God"* (Matthew 4:4).

## Frequency Determines Clarity

Your ability to hear the Spirit isn't based on His volume - it's based on your tuning. You hear what you're aligned with. *"My sheep hear my voice, and I know them, and they follow me"* (John 10:27). God doesn't speak to be figured out - He speaks to be followed. And clarity increases with obedience.

If your life is filled with contradiction, confusion, or chaos, it may not be a lack of guidance - it may be a lack of tuning. The frequency of the Spirit demands sanctification. You cannot binge Babylon and expect to hear clearly from Zion. Clarity is not a gift - it's a byproduct of consecration. *"Blessed are the pure in heart, for they shall see God."* (Matthew 5:8).

Spiritual signal is strongest in environments of holiness. The clearest ears are attached to the most surrendered hearts. *"Draw near to God, and he will draw near to you..."* (James 4:8). *"The secret of the Lord is with those who fear Him..."* (Psalm 25:14).

## The Voice Will Confront You

When the Spirit speaks, He does not coddle your compromise. He confronts it. *"When he, the Spirit of truth, comes, he will guide you into all truth…"* (John 16:13). Truth doesn't just inform - it transforms. And transformation is always violent to the flesh.

If the voice you follow never challenges your comfort, it may not be the Spirit. The Spirit will never adjust His standard to your dysfunction. He will dismantle every lie you've made room for. And in His voice is both judgment and mercy. The same voice that calls you higher will first cut you deeper. *"Is not my word like fire, declares the Lord, and like a hammer that breaks the rock in pieces?"* (Jeremiah 23:29).

He confronts your idols. He confronts your independence. He strips away excuses and exposes truth. *"All Scripture is breathed out by God and profitable for teaching, for reproof, for correction…"* (2 Timothy 3:16). *"For the word of God is living and active, sharper than any two-edged sword…"* (Hebrews 4:12).

## Spirit-Led or Self-Led

There is no neutral ground. You are either Spirit-led or self-led. The Spirit leads by fire, not formulas. *"For all who are led by the Spirit of God are sons of God"* (Romans 8:14). Sonship isn't revealed in declarations - it's proven by direction.

The self-led life is subtle. It mimics faith while resisting submission. It builds altars to its own convenience. But the Spirit-led life burns those altars and builds new ones. It doesn't need every detail - it just needs one word. When the Spirit speaks, delay is disobedience. And delayed obedience is still rebellion. *"Trust in the Lord with all your heart and lean not on your own understanding..."* (Proverbs 3:5). *"Your word is a lamp to my feet and a light to my path"* (Psalm 119:105).

To be Spirit-led is to abandon the illusion of control. *"In all your ways acknowledge Him, and He will make straight your paths"* (Proverbs 3:6).

### The Voice Creates Movement

The Spirit's voice is never idle. When He speaks, atmospheres shift, assignments awaken, and destinies accelerate. *"While they were worshiping the Lord and fasting, the Holy Spirit said, 'Set apart for me Barnabas and Saul...'"* (Acts 13:2). His voice commissions. It sends. It separates.

Many are waiting on movement while ignoring instruction. But the Voice of the Spirit is movement itself. When He speaks, you are no longer permitted to remain where you've been. You must either move or harden. His voice does not allow neutrality. It compels you toward radical surrender. *"And your ears shall hear a word behind you, saying, 'This is the way, walk in it...'"* (Isaiah 30:21).

A word from the Spirit doesn't suggest - it shifts. *"The Lord spoke to Moses, saying..."* (Exodus 25:1) - and history was never the same. The Spirit still interrupts. *"By faith Abraham obeyed when he was called to go out..."* (Hebrews 11:8).

## The Danger of Ignoring the Spirit

To ignore the Spirit is not neutral - it is rebellion. *"Do not grieve the Holy Spirit of God..."* (Ephesians 4:30). Grieving the Spirit doesn't begin with blatant sin - it begins with subtle resistance. Every time you override His whisper, your heart calcifies. Eventually, what once convicted now goes unnoticed.

The most dangerous place for a believer is not outside of church - it's inside church, with deaf ears. When the Spirit is reduced to suggestion rather than Lordship, the result is religion without power. He is not your advisor - He is your Governor. And where the Spirit of the Lord is, there must be liberty (2 Corinthians 3:17). *"They made their hearts like flint, lest they should hear the law and the words which the Lord of hosts had sent..."* (Zechariah 7:12).

*"Woe to those who are wise in their own eyes..."* (Isaiah 5:21). The more you silence the Spirit, the louder your pride becomes. *"Quench not the Spirit"* (1 Thessalonians 5:19).

## Sensitivity Must Be Guarded

Spiritual sensitivity is not sustained by emotion - it is built through devotion. *"Walk by the Spirit, and you will not gratify the desires of the flesh"* (Galatians 5:16). Every act of obedience sharpens your discernment. Every compromise dulls it.

If your heart no longer trembles when He speaks, it's time to return to the altar. Sensitivity is not a personality trait - it is a spiritual inheritance. Guard it. Fast for it. Protect it like your life depends on it - because it does. *"The Lord is near to the brokenhearted and saves the crushed in spirit"* (Psalm 34:18).

Spiritual sensitivity is developed through repetition. Every time you say yes, your ear sharpens. Every time you say no, your hearing dulls. *"Speak, Lord, for your servant is listening"* (1 Samuel 3:10). *"He awakens me morning by morning... to listen like one being instructed"* (Isaiah 50:4).

### The Voice Reveals Assignment

Your calling is not discovered through ambition. It is revealed by the Spirit. *"As many as are led by the Spirit of God, they are the sons of God"* (Romans 8:14). The voice of the Spirit is the unveiling of your scroll. It tells you who you are, where you go, and what you must release.

You do not get to choose your calling. You respond to it. The Spirit's voice will break your plans so you can enter His. And once you hear it, you cannot unhear it. His voice marks you. It ruins you for normal. It delivers you from applause and aligns you with eternal purpose. *"Call to me and I will answer you, and will tell you great and hidden things that you have not known"* (Jeremiah 33:3).

Your scroll is not activated by gifting - it is unlocked by surrender. *"Before I formed you in the womb I knew you... I appointed you a prophet to the nations"* (Jeremiah 1:5). *"The Lord God has spoken - who can but prophesy?"* (Amos 3:8).

## Conclusion: Speak, Lord - Your Servant Is Listening

The Spirit is speaking. The question is not whether He speaks - but whether you will respond. The hour demands believers who do more than hear. It demands those who tremble, who move, who surrender. The voice of the Spirit is not background noise - it is the command center of Heaven.

Let the noise of earth be silenced. Let the ears of your heart awaken. And when the Spirit speaks - move.

## Scripture Index:

- Revelation 2:7
- John 10:27
- John 16:13
- Romans 8:14
- Acts 13:2
- Ephesians 4:30
- 2 Corinthians 3:17
- Galatians 5:16
- Job 33:14

- 1 Kings 19:12
- Psalm 95:7-8
- Isaiah 30:21
- Hebrews 3:15
- Matthew 5:8
- Jeremiah 23:29
- Proverbs 3:5
- Zechariah 7:12
- Psalm 34:18

- Jeremiah 33:3
- Psalm 107:20
- James 4:8
- 2 Timothy 3:16
- Proverbs 3:6
- Exodus 25:1
- Isaiah 5:21
- 1 Samuel 3:10
- Jeremiah 1:5

- Matthew 4:4
- Psalm 25:14
- Hebrews 4:12
- Psalm 119:105
- Hebrews 11:8
- 1 Thessalonians 5:19
- Isaiah 50:4
- Amos 3:8

# Chapter Seven

## You Can't Make a Difference Until You Are Different

### Biblical Introduction: Transformation Before Impact

Before God releases a man to shift a generation, He isolates him to shape his distinction. You cannot transform what you resemble. You cannot rebuke what you mirror. You cannot lead what you refuse to leave. Scripture is clear: *"Come out from among them and be separate, says the Lord"* (2 Corinthians 6:17). Difference is not just preference - it is consecration. Before Moses ever stood before Pharaoh, he stood before a burning bush. Before David ever ruled Israel, he was shaped in solitude. And before Jesus ever launched His public ministry, He emerged from the wilderness filled with power (Luke 4:1-2, Luke 4:14).

God doesn't entrust power to those who haven't been set apart. The wilderness is not punishment - it is preparation. In the desert, God strips identity of imitation and reinforces it with revelation. *"Do not be conformed to this world, but be transformed by the renewing of your mind"* (Romans 12:2). The world shapes through pressure. Heaven shapes through presence.

Heaven never uses sameness to shift the Earth. It uses sanctified distinction. You were not born to blend. You were born to burn. Elijah burned. Jeremiah wept. John the Baptist thundered in the wilderness. All were different - set apart - not one of them could have led revival if they had settled for religious conformity. This chapter is a summons. A call to become the anomaly. The Holy disruption. The undeniable difference that Heaven can use to spark revival. You cannot make a Kingdom difference while clinging to cultural sameness. This is the cry of the Spirit: Become different.

## The Lie of Blending In

The world celebrates conformity while Heaven demands transformation. There is no anointing in imitation. There is no authority in assimilation. Many believers settle for survival in the crowd rather than distinction in the Kingdom. They crave acceptance more than anointing. But you will never make a difference if you are afraid to stand out.

"Until you find out that you're unique, you'll think you're a freak." That phrase exposes the deception of sameness. You were not made to camouflage. You were crafted to confront. Heaven did not call you to be digestible. It called you to be disruptive. Every reformer in Scripture stood alone before they stood in victory.

Blending in is not humility - it's compromise dressed in insecurity. It's easier to echo someone else's fire than to forge your own. But the Kingdom of God does not run on echoes. It advances on authentic voices. Heaven backs distinction, not duplication. *"You are the light of the world. A city set on a hill cannot be hidden"* (Matthew 5:14).

The herd mentality has plagued the Church. People want to serve God but be liked by Babylon. They want prophetic clarity without personal distinction. But to walk in your true identity, you must break the spell of normal. Difference is your inheritance. Uniformity is bondage. Sameness may earn applause, but only difference births revival.

*"Do not follow a crowd to do evil"* (Exodus 23:2). You weren't born to fit in. You were born to break through.

## Misunderstood and Marked

Being different comes with a price: misunderstanding. Jesus was despised and rejected, a man of sorrows acquainted with grief (Isaiah 53:3). Not because He failed, but because He didn't conform. When you begin to step into your divine identity, people will turn away. Family will question you. Friends will distance themselves. And religion will resist you.

But rejection is not always rejection - it's redirection into your divine lane. Rejection refines. It exposes who can walk with the oil you carry and who can't. The more marked you are by Heaven, the more misunderstood you will be on Earth. God never anoints the crowd; He anoints the consecrated.

Rejection is not a sign of failure - it is often a mark of favor. *"Woe to you when all men speak well of you, for so their fathers did to the false prophets"* (Luke 6:26). God sets apart those He intends to send. He sanctifies before He commissions. *"But when it pleased God, who separated me from my mother's womb and called me through His grace, to reveal His Son in me..."* (Galatians 1:15-16).

Difference draws warfare. Not because you're wrong, but because you're rare. You were never called to be understood - you were called to be effective. You are not abnormal. You are prophetic. You are the answer Heaven has been preparing in the secret place. And when you emerge, you will not need validation from those who overlooked you. God is your announcement.


## The Danger of Assumptions

Assumptions are the invisible prisons that contain potential. The crowd expected Elijah to look like a polished priest. He came wrapped in camel's hair. They expected Jesus to overthrow Rome; He came to overthrow sin. They expected prophets to look the part. Instead, they came looking like questions.

God breaks assumptions to birth revelation. *"What did you go out to see? A prophet? Yes, I say to you, and more than a prophet"* (Matthew 11:9). The people couldn't categorize John because John didn't fit their religious grid. And because he defied their assumptions, he became a doorway to the new.

When you break their categories, you break their control. Religious minds will always resist what they can't categorize. But

God is not raising prototypes - He's releasing originals. *"Man looks at the outward appearance, but the Lord looks at the heart"* (1 Samuel 16:7).

Don't shrink to fit their assumptions. Your distinction is not rebellion - it's revelation in motion. When God begins to reveal who you really are, the old labels lose their grip. That is when your difference becomes your doorway.

### Conversation: The First Treasure

*"We have this treasure in earthen vessels"* (2 Corinthians 4:7). The Greek word for treasure here is "thesaurus" - a collection of words. The first evidence of the treasure within you is not a platform. It's a conversation. God starts by speaking to you. And in that conversation, your true self begins to emerge.

Before God makes you visible, He makes you vocal. He talks to you until your words align with His will. Your uniqueness is unlocked through dialogue with the Divine. The treasure is not money. It's not status. It's the conversation between Heaven and your spirit.

Words from God are not casual - they are catalytic. One word from His mouth can rewrite your identity. *"Man shall not live by bread alone, but by every word that proceeds from the mouth of God"* (Matthew 4:4). Your fire doesn't start with a microphone - it starts with a whisper.

The greatest deliverance begins with the first word God speaks to you about you. And once God begins to speak, you begin to see. You see yourself differently. You see your past differently. You see your future with clarity. The conversation births distinction. And once you hear it, you cannot unhear it.

## Hyperbolē: The Grace to Go Beyond

*"That the excellence of the power may be of God and not of us"* (2 Corinthians 4:7). The word "excellence" is translated from the Greek word *hyperbolē*, meaning to throw beyond, to surpass, to exceed the mark. This is not poetic exaggeration - it is divine prophecy. You were not designed to be average. You were formed to surpass.

There is an area in your life where God intends for you to operate in *hyperbolē* - to go beyond what is normal, predictable, or expected. This is not striving - it is design. This grace doesn't come from talent or ambition. It comes from alignment. You were formed in the image of a God who exceeds. *"Now to Him who is able to do exceedingly abundantly above all that we ask or think..."* (Ephesians 3:20).

*Hyperbolē* doesn't mean you are better than others; it means you are operating in what God authored. This is the realm where your anointing fits like armor, where obedience feels like instinct, and where impact feels inevitable. You don't earn this excellence -

63

you awaken to it. It has always been embedded in your design. *"Before I formed you in the womb, I knew you"* (Jeremiah 1:5).

You are not called to rise slightly - you are called to launch supernaturally. You were not saved just to survive - you were saved to soar.

## From Image to Image: Becoming What You See

*"But we all, with unveiled face, beholding as in a mirror the glory of the Lord, are being transformed into the same image from glory to glory..."* (2 Corinthians 3:18). In the Kingdom, transformation is not accidental - it is visual. You become what you behold. The mirror of God's Word does not reflect your past - it reveals your future.

Every glimpse you catch of your future self in God's presence is a divine summons. You are being called out of what was and into what always was. Identity is not created - it is remembered. The new man is not fabricated through discipline - it is resurrected through revelation. The longer you behold His glory, the more your image is clarified, intensified, and ignited.

God doesn't upgrade your image - He restores it. He awakens what was buried beneath layers of fear, shame, religion, and culture. That is why beholding is so powerful. You're not staring into possibilities - you're staring into original blueprints.

*"For those He foreknew, He also predestined to be conformed to the image of His Son"* (Romans 8:29). That image is already encoded in you. And every encounter with glory chisels away the false layers

64

until the true image is revealed. You don't need to discover yourself - you need to behold Him.

## Permission Produces Authority

Where the Spirit of the Lord is, there is liberty (2 Corinthians 3:17). Liberty is not just emotional healing - it is Kingdom license. Heaven doesn't merely free you from bondage; it empowers you for dominion. True liberty is permission to walk fully in who God designed you to be.

Authority flows from revelation. Once Heaven reveals your identity, Hell must respect your function. *"Behold, I give you the authority to trample on serpents and scorpions"* (Luke 10:19). But authority without identity is fragile. It is rooted in performance, not position. That's why the sons of Sceva failed - because they borrowed names without carrying nature.

You don't grow into authority - you step into it. Authority is not reserved for the seasoned - it is granted to the aligned. God doesn't back experience; He backs obedience. When you receive Heaven's permission, you're not just free - you're dangerous. You become the legal enforcer of what God has written.

You don't need another title. You need divine permission. And once God says "go," you walk into atmospheres as a divine interruption. You are no longer asking the world for space - you are taking up your ordained territory.

## The Dangerous Prayer: Redefine Me

Every unique journey begins with a dangerous prayer: "Holy Spirit, redefine me." That prayer will ruin your normal. It will incinerate your pretense. It will shatter your masquerade. But in the breaking, it will awaken the blueprint.

To be redefined is to be realigned. God never asked you to polish your dysfunction. He called you to crucify it. This is not a self-help moment - it is a sacred surgery. *"Search me, O God, and know my heart... and lead me in the way everlasting"* (Psalm 139:23-24).

Redefinition means God strips away the labels that life, sin, religion, and fear wrapped around your soul. He removes titles that were never yours. He silences voices that shaped you but didn't know you. He calls you out of your camouflage and into your calling.

When you pray this prayer, Heaven doesn't just edit your life - it reveals your scroll. The sealed book begins to open. What once confused you now confronts you. What once defined you is now discarded. This is the redefinition that leads to revelation.

Hell doesn't fear your motivation. It fears your revelation. When you truly know who you are, the gates of Hell begin to shake. You become a walking contradiction to darkness. A mirror of the image of Christ. A problem Hell can't solve.

## Conclusion: The Emergence of the Different

You cannot change a world you resemble. You cannot challenge a system you are comfortable in. You must be different. Not trendy. Not weird. Prophetic. Distinct. Holy.

Difference is not rebellion. It is alignment. It is saying yes to what God wrote and no to what culture expects. *"Enter by the narrow gate... because narrow is the gate and difficult is the way which leads to life, and there are few who find it"* (Matthew 7:13-14).

Heaven is calling for anomalies - those who will disrupt the religious routine with raw obedience. Those who will exchange popularity for purity. Those who will lose the approval of men to gain the authority of Heaven. Those who will say the dangerous prayer: "Holy Spirit, show me to me."

This is your moment. The world doesn't need another echo.

It needs your voice.

It needs your difference.

It needs your emergence.

It needs you.


## Scripture Index:

- 2 Corinthians 6:17
- Luke 4:1-2,14
- Romans 12:2
- Exodus 23:2

- Isaiah 53:2-3
- Luke 6:26
- Galatians 1:15-16
- Matthew 11:7-11

- 1 Samuel 16:7

- 2 Corinthians 4:7

- Matthew 4:4

- Ephesians 3:20

- Jeremiah 1:5

- 2 Corinthians 3:17-18

- Romans 8:29

- Luke 10:19

- Psalm 139:23-24

- Matthew 7:13-14

# Chapter Eight

## The Uncommon Path

There is a road hidden in plain sight. It is not paved with popularity. It is not lit by applause. It is the path few find and fewer stay on. But it is the path where destiny breathes and scrolls unfold. The uncommon path is not reserved for the qualified - it is walked by the consecrated. This is the terrain of transformation, where Heaven trains earthborn vessels to carry divine weight. You cannot fake your way down this path. It demands all of you.

### Called Out of the Common

Every journey into purpose begins with separation. God never anoints what blends in. He calls you out - out of compromise, out of counterfeit callings, out of the comfort of being like everyone else. *"Come out from among them and be separate, says the Lord..."* (2 Corinthians 6:17). The uncommon path begins where agreement with normal ends.

You will never walk in your unique calling while clinging to common surroundings. The fire of purpose burns too hot for shallow environments. The call of God is a summons to difference. You were never created to echo culture - you were born to carry the Kingdom. *"Do not be conformed to this world, but be transformed by the renewal of your mind..."* (Romans 12:2). *"You are a chosen race, a royal priesthood, a Holy nation, a people for his own possession..."* (1 Peter 2:9).

## The Wilderness Is a Pathway

The path to the promised place always runs through the wilderness. The Spirit led Jesus into the wilderness, not the spotlight. There is no detour around dying to self. You must be stripped of applause, removed from distraction, and emptied of performance. In the wilderness, you lose what you thought mattered so God can reveal what truly does.

The wilderness is not punishment - it is preparation. It forges voice. It forges character. It reveals what you believe when you have no platform. *"Therefore, behold, I will allure her, and bring her into the wilderness, and speak tenderly to her"* (Hosea 2:14). God speaks deepest in the dry places. *"Even though I walk through the valley of the shadow of death, I will fear no evil, for you are with me..."* (Psalm 23:4). *"He humbled you and let you hunger and fed you with manna... that he might make you know that man does not live by bread alone..."* (Deuteronomy 8:3).

## The Path of Obscurity

Heaven often hides what it is preparing. Obscurity is not rejection - it is protection. When God hides you, it is because He is shaping something weighty. If you chase visibility, you'll bypass maturity. There is a process in being hidden. David killed lions and bears in fields before he ever faced Goliath in front of men.

Obscurity is not inactivity. It is sacred formation. The Lord often anoints in private before He appoints in public. *"He made my mouth like a sharp sword; in the shadow of his hand he hid me..."* (Isaiah 49:2). Those hidden by God carry authority no stage can grant. *"He who dwells in the secret place of the Most High shall abide under the shadow of the Almighty"* (Psalm 91:1). *"Truly, you are a God who hides himself..."* (Isaiah 45:15).

## The Path Demands a Yes

The uncommon path is not found - it is forged by obedience. God does not show you the full map. He gives you one word: yes. The most powerful doors are unlocked by surrender. One yielded moment can pivot your destiny. *"If you are willing and obedient, you shall eat the good of the land"* (Isaiah 1:19).

Your yes may cost you relationships. It may cost you reputation. But the reward of your yes is authority, intimacy, and eternal legacy. God does not anoint the comfortable. He anoints the surrendered. You don't need clarity to obey. You just need courage to respond. *"Trust in the Lord with all your heart and do not lean on your own understanding. In all your ways acknowledge him, and he will make straight your paths"* (Proverbs 3:5-6). *"Speak, for your servant is listening"* (1 Samuel 3:10).

## Separation Releases Revelation

God often withholds clarity until separation occurs. Abraham did not receive full instruction until he left his land. When you disconnect from what diluted you, revelation flows. The uncommon path is not walked in confusion but in faith. You walk first - then God speaks.

Revelation meets movement. Heaven waits for your step before it releases your scroll. *"Your word is a lamp to my feet and a light to my path"* (Psalm 119:105). The path may not be lit far ahead - but it's always lit under your feet. *"By faith Abraham obeyed when he was called... And he went out, not knowing where he was going"* (Hebrews 11:8). *"Call to me and I will answer you, and will tell you great and hidden things..."* (Jeremiah 33:3).

## The Uncommon Is Always Misunderstood

The moment you step onto the uncommon path, the opinions of others will rise. You will be called radical, legalistic, arrogant, or rebellious. But the Kingdom has never moved by majority vote. You cannot expect agreement from those who never heard your call.

You don't need affirmation when you have assignment. *"The natural man does not accept the things of the Spirit of God, for they are foolishness to him"* (1 Corinthians 2:14). The uncommon life will always offend common minds. You must choose obedience over optics. *"Am I now trying to win the approval of human beings, or of God?"*

(Galatians 1:10). *"Woe to you when all men speak well of you..."* (Luke 6:26).

## Pressure Produces Authenticity

The uncommon path is not easy. It is marked by pressure. But pressure reveals what comfort conceals. It is on this path that God exposes false motives, hidden insecurities, and counterfeit identities. The pressure is not to destroy you - it is to extract the purest version of you.

Gold is purified in fire. Oil is extracted through crushing. Gethsemane came before Calvary. *"We rejoice in our sufferings, knowing that suffering produces endurance, and endurance produces character..."* (Romans 5:3-4). The uncommon path does not flatter - it forges. *"The testing of your faith produces perseverance. Let perseverance finish its work..."* (James 1:3-4). *"Though he slay me, yet will I trust him..."* (Job 13:15).

## Honor in Hiddenness

On the uncommon path, you must learn to honor what is unseen. Some of your greatest victories will never be applauded by man. They happen in silence. When you say no to sin in solitude. When you obey the whisper of the Spirit when no one is watching. That is the currency of Heaven.

Man rewards performance. God rewards obedience. *"Your Father who sees in secret will reward you"* (Matthew 6:6). The unseen life is where the weight of glory rests. Never despise being hidden - it's where Heaven trains generals. *"And when you pray, go into your room and shut the door and pray to your Father who is in secret..."* (Matthew 6:6). *"For our light and momentary troubles are achieving for us an eternal glory that far outweighs them all"* (2 Corinthians 4:17).

## The Path Requires Death to Self

The uncommon path always leads to one place: the cross. You cannot carry resurrection life and preserve the old man. Something in you must die. Your ego. Your ambition. Your timelines. Until you lay it down, you cannot carry what Heaven wants to give you.

The uncommon path is not about branding - it's about burial. *"I have been crucified with Christ. It is no longer I who live, but Christ who lives in me..."* (Galatians 2:20). The cross is not symbolic - it is surgical. *"Those who belong to Christ Jesus have crucified the flesh with its passions and desires"* (Galatians 5:24). *"If anyone would come after me, let him deny himself and take up his cross daily and follow me"* (Luke 9:23).

## Few Will Follow, But Heaven Will Notice

This is not the path of crowds. It is the path of covenant. The uncommon road will not be popular, but it will be prophetic. Few will understand. Fewer will applaud. But all of Heaven watches. The cloud of witnesses leans in when a son or daughter dares to walk the narrow way.

Jesus said it clearly: *"Enter by the narrow gate. For the gate is wide and the way is easy that leads to destruction... But the gate is narrow and the way is hard that leads to life"* (Matthew 7:13-14). You will not find your scroll on the common road. It was written for the one who dares to choose the narrow. *"Many are called, but few are chosen"* (Matthew 22:14). *"For the eyes of the Lord range throughout the earth to strengthen those whose hearts are fully committed to him"* (2 Chronicles 16:9).

## Conclusion: Keep Walking

If you are on this path - don't look back. If you've stepped off - return. If you've just found it - run. There is no greater place to be than on the road God carved with His voice and marked with His blood.

This is the uncommon path. It is narrow, costly, lonely at times - but it is Holy. And it leads you to the fullness of your scroll.

## Scripture Index:

- Galatians 2:20
- Matthew 7:13-14
- Romans 12:2
- Psalm 23:4
- Psalm 91:1
- Proverbs 3:5-6
- Hebrews 11:8
- Galatians 1:10
- James 1:3-4
- Galatians 5:24
- Matthew 22:14
- 1 Peter 2:9
- Deuteronomy 8:3
- Isaiah 45:15
- 1 Samuel 3:10
- Jeremiah 33:3
- Luke 6:26
- Job 13:15
- 2 Corinthians 4:17
- Luke 9:23
- 2 Chronicles 16:9

# Chapter Nine

## You Can't Make a Difference Until You Are Different

### Biblical Introduction: Transformation Before Impact

Before God releases a man to shift a generation, He first carves him out of obscurity. You cannot transform what you resemble. You cannot deliver what you imitate. And you will never shift a culture you're still trying to belong to. "Come out from among them and be separate, says the Lord" (2 Corinthians 6:17). Before Moses ever stood before Pharaoh, he stood alone before a burning bush. Before Elijah called down fire, he stood outnumbered on Mount Carmel. Before Jesus ever opened His mouth in public ministry, He was driven into the wilderness. Why? Because power is not given to the conformed - it is given to the consecrated.

You were not born to blend in. You were born to break through. Heaven is not impressed with imitation. It backs distinction. And until you embrace the reality that you must become different, you will remain harmless in the face of darkness. This is your invitation into the wilderness of distinction - a place where God doesn't punish, but prepares. The wilderness strips off everything fake, forces confrontation with who you are, and infuses your identity with fire. It is there that God whispers the redefinition that unlocks dominion. The difference you carry must first be forged in isolation before it can explode in demonstration.

God has always used separation to prepare deliverers. Joseph was isolated in prison before he stood before Pharaoh. David was left in the pasture before he was crowned in the palace. Paul was taken into Arabia before he reshaped the Gentile world. You will never carry lasting impact if you avoid God's incubator of distinction. You must walk through the hidden place to receive Heaven's weight.

## The Lie of Blending In

The most dangerous lie in the modern Church is the subtle belief that blending in is wisdom. It isn't. It's bondage. It's the counterfeit comfort that keeps you lukewarm, invisible, and irrelevant. You cannot carry glory while craving approval. You cannot be consecrated and culturally comfortable.

"Until you find out that you're unique, you'll think you're a freak." That line reveals the war for your identity. The herd wants conformity. Heaven wants fire. You were not made to blend - you were made to burn. Elijah burned. Jeremiah wept. John the Baptist thundered. All of them were different. All of them were dangerous.

"God doesn't use sameness to shift the earth; He uses sanctified distinction." When the enemy can get you to embrace sameness, he can abort your assignment. Sameness is safe, but it is sterile. It may earn applause, but it cannot birth breakthrough. You were not meant to blend into the background of culture. You were called to erupt with the sound of your scroll.

Romans 12:2 commands, *"Do not be conformed to this world, but be transformed by the renewing of your mind."* Conformity is compromise wearing a religious badge. Transformation is Holy rebellion against Hell's patterns. When you blend in, you disarm your assignment. But when you stand out, you become a doorway to divine disruption.

The Kingdom does not advance on echoes. It advances on originals. You were not anointed to be digestible. You were anointed to disrupt. *"Do not follow a crowd to do evil"* (Exodus 23:2). You weren't born to fit in. You were born to break through. You don't need to be accepted - you need to be activated. And the moment you embrace your difference, power begins to flow.

## Misunderstood and Marked

You will never carry impact without carrying rejection. Difference is a burden before it becomes a blessing. *"He was despised and rejected by men, a man of sorrows and acquainted with grief"* (Isaiah 53:3). Heaven's favorites are often earth's outcasts. That's the price of being marked.

You can't be commissioned until you've been separated. Rejection is not rejection - it's redirection. God is not preparing you to be popular; He's preparing you to be powerful. People won't understand your oil because they didn't see your crushing. You don't need validation when God has given you vision.

"Rejection is not an accident; it's a sign of favor." Many won't understand the transformation happening in you because it confronts the compromise still alive in them. You will be misunderstood, avoided, labeled, and isolated. But God uses rejection to prune your audience. Everyone can't handle your oil. When God separates, He sanctifies. And when He sanctifies, He qualifies.

Jesus warned in John 15:19, *"If you were of the world, the world would love its own. Yet because you are not of the world... the world hates you."* Rejection is a mark of separation, and separation is a prerequisite for elevation. You cannot step into divine power without first stepping out of human acceptance.

Hell resists what Heaven has marked. The warfare is not against your potential - it's against your becoming. You are not strange. You are selected. And when your moment comes, you won't need to announce yourself - your difference will do it for you.

## The Danger of Assumptions

Assumptions are prisons. They are invisible chains that limit divine expression. When John the Baptist emerged, they didn't know what to do with him. *"What did you go out to see? A prophet? Yes, and more than a prophet"* (Matthew 11:9). He didn't fit their religious box. That's why he was powerful.

"Assumptions are the graves of destiny." When people assume what you're supposed to be, they try to confine what God is still defining. John didn't come to fulfill their categories. He came to break them. And so will you.

Your uniqueness will offend religious minds. They wanted Elijah, but they got John. They expected a warrior, but they got a wild man. Heaven always sends anomalies to break assumptions. Don't shrink to fit their small categories. Your distinction is a weapon. Let God break every box they tried to put you in.

When David showed up to face Goliath, Saul assumed he needed armor. But David knew his difference was his advantage. He rejected Saul's armor and chose his sling (1 Samuel 17:39-40). The world will try to dress you in expectation, but God will clothe you in authenticity. You are not a repeat. You are not a remix. You are an original. The moment you defy their assumptions, you become a doorway to the new.

## Conversation: The First Treasure

*"We have this treasure in earthen vessels"* (2 Corinthians 4:7). That treasure is not fame. It is not applause. It is conversation. The Greek word for treasure is "thesaurus" - a collection of words. Your first evidence of divine design is the conversation God starts having with you.

Before God uses your voice, He adjusts your vocabulary. Before He gives you a stage, He gives you a secret place. The whisper comes before the microphone. If you don't have a word from Heaven, don't expect authority on Earth. When God speaks, He releases your identity.

"The greatest evidence of calling is not a platform - it's a conversation." It is in that whisper that your original identity begins to emerge. You were not called to impress crowds. You were called to carry a sound that pierces darkness. And that sound is forged in secret when Heaven speaks to your spirit.

In Matthew 4:4, Jesus declares, *"Man shall not live by bread alone, but by every word that proceeds from the mouth of God."* Your survival, strength, and significance are tied to divine conversation. One word can realign you. One whisper can reroute your destiny. You don't find your voice in public. You find it in private. The treasure is not external success - it is internal alignment. One word from God can recalibrate decades of confusion.

## Hyperbolē: The Grace to Go Beyond

There is a grace on your life to exceed the average. *"That the excellence (hyperbolē) of the power may be of God and not of us"* (2 Corinthians 4:7). You were not born to match the status quo. You were born to surpass it. Heaven didn't create you to meet the standard - it designed you to redefine it.

Hyperbolē means to throw beyond the line. There is a specific area of your life where God has graced you to go further than others. Not in pride. Not in ego. But in design. It's not ambition. It's assignment. It is the God-implanted capacity to exceed limitations. It's the evidence of divine intentionality. *"Now to Him who is able to do exceedingly abundantly above all that we ask or think..."* (Ephesians 3:20). That is hyperbolē in motion.

You were created in the image of a limitless God. Therefore, your design carries the DNA of acceleration. This doesn't mean you'll be applauded - it means you'll be attacked. But breakthrough isn't birthed in safe places. It's born in the place where you outgrow the boundaries others try to impose on your calling.

This is the place where your anointing fits like armor. Where obedience feels like instinct. Where impact feels inevitable. You were never meant to function in neutral. You are Heaven's velocity in human form. You are not merely running the race - you are breaking records.

## From Image to Image: Becoming What You See

*"But we all, with unveiled face, beholding as in a mirror the glory of the Lord, are being transformed into the same image from glory to glory..."* (2 Corinthians 3:18). In the Kingdom, you become what you behold. Transformation is visual before it is behavioral. Revelation precedes reformation.

83

God is not updating your personality - He's revealing your prototype. Every glimpse of His glory is a mirror of your true identity. *"For those He foreknew, He also predestined to be conformed to the image of His Son"* (Romans 8:29). That image is already encoded in you. Every encounter chisels away the dust of deception to reveal what was there all along.

This is not behavior modification. It is identity resurrection. It's not about effort - it's about exposure. When you behold Him, you see you. When you worship, you awaken. Beholding is the invitation to become.

Moses didn't glow from climbing the mountain. He glowed from beholding the glory. Your change doesn't come from striving - it comes from seeing. You become the image you gaze upon. That is why Hell wants you distracted, discouraged, and disoriented - because if you ever see Him clearly, you'll never walk the same again.

## Permission Produces Authority

*"Where the Spirit of the Lord is, there is liberty"* (2 Corinthians 3:17). Liberty is not a feeling - it is a license. Heaven doesn't just free you from bondage; it grants you jurisdiction. You are not just delivered - you are deputized.

Luke 10:19 confirms this: *"Behold, I give you the authority to trample on serpents and scorpions, and over all the power of the enemy."* But authority without identity becomes fragile. The sons of Sceva had language, but no license. They tried to use a name they hadn't been aligned with. And they were humiliated (Acts 19:13-16).

Heaven only backs what it authors. You don't grow into authority through time - you access it through revelation. "God doesn't back experience - He backs obedience." The moment you receive divine permission, you step into divine dominion. You no longer ask for space - you occupy it.

Authority is not volume - it's validation. It's not charisma - it's covenant. And once you know who you are, the gates of Hell recognize it. You become a legal enforcer, not a passive believer. Your voice carries the backing of the Throne.

## The Dangerous Prayer: Redefine Me

Every transformation begins with a dangerous prayer: "Holy Spirit, redefine me." That prayer ruins the masquerade. It dismantles every false construct you've used for safety. It shatters the labels placed by parents, pastors, culture, and shame.

*"Search me, O God, and know my heart; try me and know my anxieties. And see if there is any wicked way in me, and lead me in the way everlasting"* (Psalm 139:23-24). This isn't just a prayer of inspection - it's a summons to excavation. Redefinition is the death of the imposter and the resurrection of the original.

You cannot make a Kingdom difference if you're clinging to cultural definitions. This prayer is a Holy surrender. It means letting God burn the scripts that no longer fit your scroll. It means yielding to a revelation that offends your reputation.

"God will not anoint who you pretend to be." He can only empower what He designed. And when you let Him redefine you, you recover the power of your original name - the one written in the Lamb's book before time began.

## Conclusion: The Emergence of the Different

Heaven is not calling for more copies. It is crying out for anomalies. You cannot change what you resemble. You must become the contradiction. The Holy disruption. The divine anomaly.

Jesus didn't die to make you polite. He died to make you powerful. You were not saved to blend. You were saved to burn. This is your moment of confrontation. If you keep hiding in the herd, you will never hear Heaven say, "Well done."

Matthew 7:14 declares, *"Narrow is the gate and difficult is the way which leads to life, and there are few who find it."* This journey is not for the crowd - it's for the called. Few will pay the price to be different. But those few will alter the course of history.

Lift your hands and pray it again:

"Holy Spirit, redefine me. Show me to me. I am ready to become what You wrote."

Because the world doesn't need another echo. It needs your voice. It needs your emergence. It needs you.

**Scripture References:**

- 2 Corinthians 6:17
- Isaiah 53:3
- Matthew 11:9
- 2 Corinthians 4:7
- Exodus 23:2
- Ephesians 3:20
- Romans 8:29
- Luke 10:19
- 2 Corinthians 3:17-18
- Psalm 139:23-24
- John 15:19
- 1 Samuel 17:39-40
- Matthew 4:4
- Acts 19:13-16
- Matthew 7:14

# Chapter Ten

## The Power of Identity Memory

### Biblical Introduction: The Call to Remember

God does not ask His people to remember because He forgets. He commands remembrance because we do. Identity in the Kingdom is not only a matter of revelation but of retention. The battle over your identity is often waged through the weapon of forgetfulness. The Spirit of God repeatedly issues this charge throughout Scripture: "Remember." Not just to recall an event, but to re-anchor identity. "Remember who you are. Remember who I am. Remember what I said." When you forget, you drift. When you remember, you align. Deuteronomy 8 is not nostalgia - it is a prophetic safeguard. *"Beware that you do not forget the LORD your God..."* (Deuteronomy 8:11). Forgetfulness is more than mental lapse; it is spiritual sabotage.

### The Spirit of Forgetfulness

For many, the greatest enemy of purpose is not the devil. It's forgetfulness. Not amnesia of facts, but of design. The Spirit of Forgetfulness robs believers of clarity and confidence. It's not simply that they forget Scripture - they forget self. They forget what God spoke in the secret place. They forget what was branded in tears and confirmed by miracles. They forget the word that sustained them in the valley.

"The devil doesn't always need to steal your gift; he just needs you to forget you have it." And in that subtle deception, lives drift from scroll to script, from revelation to repetition. Forgetfulness is how gifted people become functional but fruitless. They still go to church. Still volunteer. Still quote verses. But they forget the fire. They forget the promise. They forget the war they already won.

To be sedated by the familiar is to forfeit the supernatural. And many are walking in circles, not because they are disobedient, but because they are forgetful. The Spirit of Forgetfulness functions as a veil over the soul, clouding the memory of covenant. Psalm 106:21 declares, *"They forgot God their Savior, who had done great things in Egypt."* It wasn't that God stopped being God; it was that they ceased to remember.

**The Role of Memory in Spiritual Identity**

Memory is not mental; it's prophetic. It is the echo chamber of identity. What you remember defines what you pursue. Identity must be reinforced to be sustained. When God speaks, it's not just to reveal - it's to imprint. Every word from Heaven is a seed of identity.

God reminded Abraham of his name. He reminded Moses of his calling. He reminded Joshua of the promise. *"Only be strong and very courageous... remember the word that Moses my servant commanded you"* (Joshua 1:7, Joshua 1:13). Memory in the Kingdom is not nostalgia; it's navigation. Without it, you lose direction.

You do not grow by forgetting. You grow by remembering who you are in the Spirit. Revelation without retention leads to religious performance without prophetic posture. That's why Hell doesn't just fight your future; it erases your memory of your divine past.

Paul, writing to Timothy, said, *"Stir up the gift of God which is in you through the laying on of my hands"* (2 Timothy 1:6). That stirring is not new impartation - it is remembered identity. It is the Spirit shaking awake what has gone dormant. True identity is sustained not through emotion, but repetition.

## How Israel Forgot Who They Were

Israel did not fall because of a lack of miracles. They fell because they forgot the One who performed them. In Exodus, they walked through parted seas. In Numbers, they ate Heaven-baked bread. Yet by Deuteronomy, they are warned not to forget.

They forgot their deliverance. They forgot their design. They forgot their identity. They wanted a king like the nations, forgetting they had a King like no other. They melted down their memory of the mountain and made a golden calf in its place.

Forgetfulness created their fall. Memory would have preserved their dominion. Their loss was not due to power shortage but identity erosion. *"They forgot His works and the wonders He had shown them"* (Psalm 78:11). When you forget God's history with you, you rewrite your destiny without Him.

In Judges 8:34, Scripture says, *"The children of Israel did not remember the LORD their God, who had delivered them from the hands of all their enemies."* Their forgetfulness became a generational curse. Forgetfulness becomes spiritual generational decay. The moment identity is forgotten, idolatry is invited.

## Why God Told Them to Build Memorials

God didn't need stones. He needed memory. When the Jordan River dried up for Israel to cross, God commanded Joshua to gather twelve stones from the riverbed and build a memorial. *"That this may be a sign among you... when your children ask... then you shall answer"* (Joshua 4:6-7).

Memorials are not about monuments - they are altars of identity. They shout to future generations, "We didn't get here by accident." Every testimony is a bridge to identity. Every stone is a sermon.

He told them to write the law on the doorposts. Bind it to their hands. Talk of it when they walk, sit, and lie down. Why? Because identity is fragile without memory. Your miracle must become your meditation, or it will be stolen by the next crisis.

God's command in Deuteronomy 6:6-9 was strategic: *"These words which I command you today shall be in your heart... you shall bind them as a sign on your hand... write them on the doorposts of your house."* When the Word is in sight, memory stays in strength.

## Personal Identity Markers in Scripture

God often renamed His people to anchor their identity in memory. Abram became Abraham. Sarai became Sarah. Jacob became Israel. Saul became Paul. The name change wasn't cosmetic. It was covenantal. It was a memorial in their very identity.

*"You shall no longer be called Abram, but Abraham, for I have made you a father of many nations"* (Genesis 17:5). Your name is Heaven's memory stamp. It carries your design, not just your designation.

When God changes your name, He imprints your future onto your memory. You cannot go back to who you were when Heaven starts calling you who you are.

Isaiah 62:2 speaks to prophetic renaming: *"You shall be called by a new name, which the mouth of the LORD shall name."* When Heaven speaks a new name over you, Hell loses the right to call you by the old one.

## Forgetfulness as a Form of Spiritual Warfare

This is not a mental battle. It is spiritual warfare. Satan is not afraid of your church attendance. He's terrified of your memory. Because memory leads to authority. *"Bless the LORD, O my soul, and forget not all His benefits"* (Psalm 103:2). When you forget, you forfeit.

The enemy will seduce you to forget your testimony, your encounter, your promise. Because when you forget your scroll, you stop walking in it. You begin to live off imitation instead of impartation.

To win the war over your life, you must win the war for your memory. This is why the enemy attacks with distraction, offense, and exhaustion. If he can't destroy your identity, he will delete your memory of it.

Jesus, in the wilderness, overcame the enemy by remembering the Word: *"It is written..."* (Matthew 4:4). He didn't quote new revelation; He recalled ancient truth. Memory is a weapon. And when it is wielded with faith, demons flee.

## The Return of Identity Through Remembrance

Identity is not invented - it is remembered. It is excavated from past visitations, from old journals, from forgotten prophecies. The return to identity is the return to remembrance.

*"I will remember the works of the LORD: surely I will remember thy wonders of old"* (Psalm 77:11). Your memory is a map. Go back to where God first met you. Revisit the place of your awakening. Reread the page where Heaven wrote your name.

Remembrance is not passive. It is prophetic. It stirs your soul. It reactivates what went dormant. It reminds you what Hell tried to bury.

Jesus said to the church in Ephesus, *"Remember therefore from where you have fallen; repent and do the first works"* (Revelation 2:5). Revival begins with remembrance. Restoration begins with remembering your first love.

## Prophetic Memory: Remembering the Scroll

You were not born to improvise. You were born to align with the scroll written before time. Your scroll is not a metaphor - it is a mandate. *"In the volume of the book it is written of me, I delight to do your will, O God"* (Psalm 40:7-8).

Prophetic memory is when God shows you the page you forgot. It is the Holy Spirit awakening your spirit to the assignment you stopped pursuing. Your scroll doesn't change. But you can forget it.

When memory returns, so does momentum. Your destiny is not ahead of you. It's inside of you, waiting for remembrance to unlock it.

Hebrews 10:7 affirms the scroll: *"Then I said, 'Behold, I have come - in the volume of the book it is written of Me - to do Your will, O God."* This is not a poetic phrase. It is a revelation of Heaven's script written for your life.

## Deuteronomy 8 and the Warning Against Amnesia

Deuteronomy 8 is a solemn charge to remember. God says: *"Beware that you do not forget the LORD your God... lest when you have eaten and are full... then your heart is lifted up, and you forget"* (Deuteronomy 8:11-14).

Spiritual amnesia is lethal. It leads to pride, disobedience, and idolatry. God warns that forgetfulness is the gateway to destruction. Memory is not a luxury - it is a spiritual necessity.

Remember where you came from. Remember the wilderness. Remember the manna. Remember the miracles. Memory is how you stay grounded when you get promoted.

The Lord concludes the chapter with a chilling word: *"If you ever forget the LORD your God and follow other Gods... you shall surely perish"* (Deuteronomy 8:19). To forget God is to forfeit life.

## The Book of Remembrance in Malachi

*"Then those who feared the LORD spoke to one another, and the LORD listened and heard them; so a book of remembrance was written before Him"* (Malachi 3:16). God keeps a book of memory. And every time you honor Him, He writes it down.

You're not forgotten. Your obedience is recorded. Your sacrifice is written. God remembers what men forget. And your identity is preserved in His remembrance.

Heaven has a filing system for Worshippers. The Book of Remembrance isn't poetry. It is proof. You have not labored in vain.

95

Hebrews 6:10 confirms this: *"For God is not unjust to forget your work and labor of love."* Your history with God is never lost. Every private obedience is permanently inscribed in the eternal ledger of Heaven.

## Memory as a Weapon for Destiny

Memory is not just reflection - it is a weapon. When David faced Goliath, he didn't reference armor. He referenced memory. *"The LORD who delivered me from the paw of the lion and the bear will deliver me from this Philistine"* (1 Samuel 17:37).

David didn't need a new word - he needed a remembered one. What you recall in the battle determines how you fight. Your memory gives your slingshot precision.

When the enemy comes with intimidation, strike him with remembrance. Recall your history with God. Remember your victories. Declare your scroll.

Psalm 119:52 says, *"I remembered Your judgments of old, O LORD, and have comforted myself."* Remembrance is how warriors stabilize their spirit in the storm. You cannot wage war without a prophetic memory.

## Memory and the Power of Testimony

Testimony is the echo of memory wrapped in worship. It is a public declaration of a private miracle. *"They overcame him by the blood of the Lamb and by the word of their testimony"* (Revelation 12:11).

Testimony stirs up memory and memory stirs up momentum. Every time you testify, you remind yourself and others that God has moved before - and He will move again.

"Your testimony is your sword. Your memory is your map. Your identity is your armor. And your scroll is your strategy." You were never meant to live in the fog of forgetfulness. You were meant to burn with the fire of remembrance.

Psalm 105:1-5 urges us, *"Give thanks to the LORD, call upon His name; make known His deeds... Remember His marvelous works which He has done."* Your testimony is not just for celebration - it's for war.

## Conclusion: The Recovery of Identity Is the Return of Memory

Heaven is not calling you to invent yourself. Heaven is calling you to remember who you are. You are not starting over. You are returning to your scroll. To your name. To your design. The power of identity is not discovery - it is remembrance.

So lift your hands. Say it aloud. Declare it with fire: "Holy Spirit, awaken my memory. Let me remember what You wrote. Show me who I was before the world told me who I had to be."

Remembrance is revival. And the power of your identity is waiting to be remembered.

**Scripture Index:**

# Chapter Eleven

## The Danger of Assumptions

### Introduction: Confronting False Images

What you assume about yourself can become the greatest enemy to what God declared over you. Assumptions aren't always formed from rebellion - they're often built in religion. But religious assumptions are more lethal than worldly lies because they cloak themselves in God's language while denying His revelation. The ones who should have recognized Christ missed Him - not because He lacked power, but because He shattered their assumptions (John 1:10-11).

Jesus asked three times, *"What did you go out to see?"* (Matthew 11:7-9). Not because He was confused - but because they were. They expected a reed swaying with the wind, a man in soft garments, a prophet like the old ones. But what stood before them was a Holy disruption - a new standard. The greatest ever born of a woman stood in camel's hair and locust breath. Heaven had redefined the prophetic, but their assumptions blocked the revelation.

The same question echoes today: What did you go out to see? A leader wrapped in titles? A ministry styled for applause? A calling that mirrors your neighbor's? If your answer is built on borrowed expectations, you're already misaligned. You will miss the move of God if you're married to a model He never endorsed.

## The Invisible Prison of Presumption

Religious assumptions are subtle tyrants. They don't yell - they whisper. They embed themselves in your language, your doctrine, your definitions of what success, anointing, and calling should look like. And then they imprison you (Mark 7:13).

"Most of the church world lives in assumptions." They think they're walking in faith, but they're functioning in a formula. Assumptions taught them that prophets had to sound like Elijah, apostles had to look like Peter, and evangelists had to wear suits and shout in stadiums. They worship a mold and crucify the emergence of anything that doesn't fit inside it.

Jesus asked three times, *"What did you go out to see?"* (Matthew 11:7-9). The repetition wasn't redundancy - it was revelation. Heaven was recalibrating expectation. Those trapped in tradition couldn't recognize the new, because their vision was held hostage by the old.

Many today have assumed that the move of God must come dressed in the same language, form, and flow of the past. They believe the only valid expressions of power must mirror previous revivals or religious norms. But the God who split the Red Sea (Exodus 14:21-22) and who came wrapped in flesh (John 1:14) will not be contained in the box of human tradition. If your

100

calling must look like someone else's in order to feel legitimate, you are not walking in calling - you're living in cloning. Break the mold or the mold will break you. The Spirit of God is not recycling; He is revealing.

## John the Baptist: God's Rebuke to Assumptions

John didn't fit the system, so he became the sign. He didn't echo the Old Testament prophets in miracles - but Jesus called him the greatest. Why? Because greatness isn't always proven by display. It's measured by alignment (Luke 7:28).

Heaven was announcing a new move of God through John, and the people didn't know what to do with it. They were looking for Elijah's fire, Moses' rod, or Isaiah's poetry. What they got was a wild man with a message that burned. He shattered every assumption - and for that, he became Heaven's doorway.

When you carry something God has never released before, you will never fit the stereotypes. People will compare you to what they've seen because it's all they know. But comparison is the language of those who lack revelation (2 Corinthians 10:12).

John was not a prototype of religious comfort; he was a disruption to religious conformity. He wore garments that made people uncomfortable. He baptized with boldness and rebuked with fire. And yet Jesus said, *"Among those born of women there has not risen anyone greater than John the Baptist"* (Matthew 11:11). This is proof that Heaven does not measure greatness by what impresses men - but by what aligns with the scroll. If you are waiting to be recognized by familiar models, you may miss the very anointing that sets you apart.

### The Report of the Lord vs. The Opinion of the Herd

*"Who has believed our report?"* (Isaiah 53:1). The question still pierces the air. The report is not about your behavior. It's about your identity. It's about what God wrote before anyone else formed an opinion (Jeremiah 1:5).

Many have opted to believe the opinion of the herd rather than the report of the Lord. They chose safety over sanctification, applause over assignment. "I want to be safe. I don't want to take chances." That mindset will keep you blending when Heaven called you to break through.

Let it echo in your soul: You cannot be safe and be unique at the same time in the herd. Step out. Cut off whatever is pulling you back into comfort. There's a pioneer in you, and pioneers never stay where settlers are satisfied.

God's report declares you righteous, chosen, anointed, and sent (1 Peter 2:9). The opinion of the herd says you must conform, perform, and stay small to be accepted. But obedience to God's report often means you will stand alone before you lead others. Noah believed the report and built an ark in a drought (Hebrews 11:7). Abraham believed and left his homeland (Genesis 12:1-4). Mary believed and birthed what had never existed (Luke 1:38). The report always demands risk. But that risk is the soil of legacy.

## Root Out of Dry Ground

Isaiah prophesied of Jesus, *"He grew up before Him like a tender shoot, and like a root out of dry ground"* (Isaiah 53:2). The picture is powerful. A barren desert. Cracked soil. No signs of life. Then suddenly, a tree breaks through the crust. That's you.

"There's nobody going to be quite like you." And that's by design. Your uniqueness is your fingerprint from Heaven. It will not always be understood, but it must be obeyed. The first person to recognize your design may not even be you. But it is emerging - and it is prophetic.

When you begin to think differently, see differently, feel like you don't fit - it's not dysfunction. It's distinction. You are a seed Heaven planted in dry ground to announce something new.

Do not underestimate the power of your emergence in a dry place. Your breakthrough is not just personal - it is prophetic. You were planted in a barren land so your growth would prophesy rain (Joel 2:23). You were designed to rise in the unlikely place, to become the contradiction to every dry, dead thing around you. Your very life becomes a message: *"He still brings life where there was none"* (Ezekiel 37:5). And that is the power of your difference.

## Redefining What a Move of God Looks Like

Some of the greatest moves of God don't look spiritual on the surface. The man who started the Power Team - breaking bricks and ice blocks - looked foolish to the religious elite. But he filled arenas and brought people to Christ.

The move of God on your life won't make sense to those who've only known one model. They will laugh. They will question. They will say, "Are there prophets today?" They did it in Jesus' day - and they'll do it in yours (Matthew 13:57). Don't let their skepticism redefine your scroll.

God is not asking for permission to do something new through you. He's asking for obedience. He's calling you to believe your own report, even if no one else does. He's saying, "Are you even listening for the report, or are you just part of the herd?"

When God begins to move, it rarely fits within the frame of past experiences. When He moved through David, it looked like a sling, not a sword (1 Samuel 17:40). When He moved through the early Church, it looked like tongues, not titles (Acts 2:4). When He moves through you, it may look like business, art, technology, or strategy. But do not confuse unfamiliarity with unspirituality. Obedience is the new wine skin (Mark 2:22).

## Assumptions Will Cost You Everything

Assumptions about what you can and cannot do, about who you are or aren't, will cost you everything Heaven wrote about you. They will bind your identity in religious wrapping and call it obedience. But it's not obedience - it's delay.

You've got to come out. You've got to leave the herd behind. You've got to silence the voices that mock your difference and step into the assignment that can't be cloned. Let the mockers laugh. Let the settlers settle. You are a pioneer.

Let this truth ignite you: "You can't be a pioneer if you stay in the herd." Pioneers don't follow the path - they forge it. They don't echo the past - they introduce the future.

Assumptions are often cloaked in logic, but Heaven doesn't run on logic - it runs on Lordship (Proverbs 3:5-6). The assumptions that seem safest are often the ones that silence you. Saul assumed David needed his armor (1 Samuel 17:38-39). Israel assumed the Messiah would overthrow Rome (Luke 24:21). The Pharisees assumed authority came from age and title (John 7:15). But those assumptions became tombs for truth. If you want to fulfill the scroll God wrote, you must murder the assumptions that Hell planted.

## Conclusion: A Dangerous Question for a Dangerous Generation

Jesus didn't ask "What did you go out to see?" for trivia. He asked it to shatter illusions. He asked it to prepare a people for what had never been seen before. He is asking the same now.

What did you expect to become? What did you assume your calling would look like? Whose voice shaped your definition of purpose? If your assumptions are still in control, your calling is still in captivity.

But if you're willing - truly willing - to let Heaven interrupt your assumptions, then prepare to emerge as something the world's never seen before. You are not called to blend in. You are not called to repeat. You are called to disrupt. To redefine. To become.

## Scripture Index:

- John 1:10-11
- Matthew 11:7-11
- Mark 7:13
- Exodus 14:21-22
- John 1:14
- Luke 7:28
- 2 Corinthians 10:12
- Isaiah 53:1-2
- Jeremiah 1:5
- 1 Peter 2:9
- Hebrews 11:7
- Genesis 12:1-4

- Luke 1:38
- Joel 2:23
- Ezekiel 37:5
- Matthew 13:57
- 1 Samuel 17:40,
- 1 Samuel 38-39
- Acts 2:4
- Mark 2:22
- Proverbs 3:5-6
- Luke 24:21
- John 7:15

# Chapter Twelve

## Becoming the Evidence

### Biblical Introduction:  Heaven Is Looking for Witnesses

Every generation is given signs, wonders, and sermons. But what God longs for most is evidence - living proof of His intent, His nature, and His power. Not a polished performance, but an incarnated truth. *"You are My witnesses,"* says the Lord (Isaiah 43:10). A witness does not recite hearsay - they speak from firsthand encounter.  Heaven is not recruiting parrots - it is raising prototypes. Your life is not meant to simply echo theology. It is meant to embody a scroll.

God is searching the earth, not just for worshippers in spirit and in truth - but for sons and daughters who bear His image so boldly, so unashamedly, that they become the message. The evidence is not found in religious routine - it is discovered in radical obedience. You don't just carry an assignment - you are the assignment. You are not only carrying evidence. You are called to become it.

### Evidence Over Explanation

The world doesn't need more explanations. It needs evidence. It needs people who don't just talk about breakthrough -

they walk in it. Who don't quote authority - they exercise it. *"The Kingdom of God is not in word but in power"* (1 Corinthians 4:20).

You were never meant to merely defend the truth. You were designed to demonstrate it. That's why Hell isn't threatened by information - it's terrified of transformation. A man on fire needs no introduction. He is the message (Jeremiah 20:9).

The problem with modern Christianity is that it produces explainers, not evidencers. Sermons are crafted but lives remain unchanged. We've learned how to preach about deliverance while remaining bound. We've learned how to host conferences about identity while still walking in insecurity. That's not the gospel - that's performance.

God is raising up believers whose very existence contradicts the culture. Whose nature carries evidence of the unseen Kingdom. Not just those who can articulate doctrine - but those who carry undeniable proof that the gospel is alive. They don't just preach freedom - they live it. They don't just talk about joy - they emanate it. They don't quote healing - they walk whole (Galatians 5:22-23).

These evidencers don't simply agree with doctrine - they provoke transformation. Their silence convicts. Their lifestyle convicts. Their resilience under pressure convicts. They are mirrors of a world not seen, a people not formed in religion but forged in revelation. When they walk in, systems bend and atmospheres answer.

## You Are the Scroll

Every person born of God has a scroll - a prewritten volume that contains their divine assignment (Psalm 40:7-8). But the scroll is not just to be read. It's to be embodied. You are not called to simply teach what God said - you are called to become what He wrote.

Jesus didn't just bring a message. He was the message. *"The Word became flesh and dwelt among us"* (John 1:14). In the same way, the prophetic words spoken over your life must become flesh in you. You are the manifestation of a hidden manuscript. Your obedience is what turns prophecy into presence (Hebrews 10:7).

Your identity is not a theory. It's a scroll waiting to be worn. And when you begin to live from the reality of what God wrote, you stop asking for confirmation - you become confirmation. You are not waiting on a sign. You are the sign (Isaiah 8:18).

The scroll you carry is not fictional - it is factual in Heaven. It's not a hopeful dream - it's a divine blueprint. And when you live in contradiction to it, frustration becomes inevitable. Heaven cannot finance what it did not author. The favor of God follows those who step into what was written.

Every time you compromise with culture, you betray your scroll. Every time you dilute your fire, you mute your mandate. Your scroll carries Kingdom weight, and it demands Kingdom posture. You are not a motivational speaker with scripture. You are a scroll that walks.

## Walking Proof in a Skeptical World

We live in an age that demands proof but mocks the process. People want power but reject consecration. They want Kingdom results without Kingdom surrender. That's why God is not looking for celebrities - He's looking for witnesses. Witnesses who bleed truth. Who shake atmospheres. Who bear fruit that cannot be denied.

*"By their fruit you will know them"* (Matthew 7:20). Not by their words. Not by their followers. Not by their aesthetics. Fruit is the evidence. And fruit is not manufactured - it's birthed from intimacy (John 15:4-5).

Your life was never meant to be an argument. It was meant to be evidence. The most powerful apologetic is a life transformed by grace and rooted in design. You are God's answer to culture's confusion. Not because you know more - but because you've become more.

To be walking proof is to be allergic to compromise. It means refusing to shrink so others feel safe. It means living with the kind of clarity that exposes every counterfeit. You are not called to explain yourself - you're called to display Him (Philippians 2:15).

God will not apologize for your distinction. He will not soften your edge to make others comfortable. Your holiness is offensive to the religious. Your fire is a threat to the lukewarm. But that is the cost of carrying fruit in a barren generation.

## Hell Fears the Evidence

The enemy is not afraid of your attendance - he's afraid of your evidence. Because once you become evidence, you're no longer controllable. You're no longer manipulated by shame, silenced by fear, or bound by comparison. You have become the embodiment of the threat.

When Jesus raised Lazarus, the religious leaders didn't just plot against Jesus - they plotted against Lazarus. *"For on account of him, many of the Jews were going away and believing in Jesus"* (John 12:11). Lazarus was evidence. And evidence must be silenced.

You are not dangerous to Hell because of your gifting. You're dangerous because of your transformation. A changed life is the loudest sermon. A delivered soul is the loudest roar. You are Hell's reminder that the grave doesn't win. That shame doesn't last. That identity can be resurrected (Revelation 12:11).

This is why the fight intensified after your breakthrough. Because now you're not just hearing truth - you've become it. You're not just quoting promises - you've become the proof.

Evidence terrifies Hell because it invalidates every lie. When you walk into a room healed, whole, and Holy, every demon is reminded of its failure. You are Hell's failed project. Its lost investment. Its loudest loss. And that's why warfare follows transformation - because evidence can't be explained away.

### When Evidence Walks In

When evidence walks into a room, atmospheres shift. Chains react. Darkness trembles. Because authority has shown up - not in theory, but in form. You are not just a carrier of the Kingdom. You are its evidence.

You were born to be a walking contradiction to the system. A divine interruption to the demonic cycle. Your voice, your decisions, your posture - everything about you becomes a living protest against the ordinary. You are the rebuttal to Hell's accusations. The evidence that grace doesn't just cover - it transforms (2 Corinthians 5:17).

You don't need to announce your anointing when you are evidence. Doors open. Demons flee. People weep. Not because of your presentation - but because of your presence. You don't have to prove anything. Your life proves it all.

This is why you can't afford to live distracted. You are not on Earth to survive. You are here to bear witness. When evidence walks into a boardroom, it carries revival. When it walks into a broken home, it brings reconciliation. When it enters a classroom, it births awakening. Evidence walks in, and Heaven has legal access.

## Evidence Will Cost You

Becoming evidence is not free. It will cost you comfort. It will cost you reputation. It may cost you relationships. But what it produces is eternal. *"For I consider that the sufferings of this present time are not worthy to be compared with the glory that is to be revealed in us"* (Romans 8:18).

Evidence is not born in comfort - it is forged in fire. It is shaped in crushing. You don't get to carry this weight without dying to the version of you that lived for applause. If you want to be evidence, you must surrender your addiction to affirmation (Luke 9:23-24).

God is not asking you to be impressive. He is asking you to be incarnate. To wear the word. To live the message. To carry the weight of a truth so heavy it can't be faked. That's why your path is different. That's why your journey feels longer. You're not being delayed - you're being deepened.

You can't become evidence and stay invisible. You can't become evidence and stay passive. When you say yes to becoming the evidence, Heaven marks you. And Hell targets you. But glory surrounds you.

Every scar becomes a sermon. Every loss becomes leverage. Every silence becomes strategy. And every tear becomes testimony. This is the price of being a witness: you become what others refuse to carry. You wear the proof they only preach.

## Conclusion: The Scroll Must Walk

You are not here to explain the Kingdom. You are here to express it. To be the sign. The wonder. The contradiction. The fulfillment of what was spoken in shadows now walking in the light. You are the scroll God is unrolling before a watching world.

You don't need to become popular. You need to become proof. The earth is groaning for it. Creation is waiting for it. And Heaven has invested too much in you for you to hide now. The time for mere declarations is over. The time to become has come.

You are the evidence.

## Scripture Index:

- Isaiah 43:10
- 1 Corinthians 4:20
- Psalm 40:7-8
- John 1:14
- Hebrews 10:7
- Isaiah 8:18
- Matthew 7:20
- John 15:4-5

- Philippians 2:15
- John 12:11
- Revelation 12:11
- 2 Corinthians 5:17
- Romans 8:18
- Luke 9:23-24
- Galatians 5:22-23
- Jeremiah 20:9

# Chapter Thirteen

## Walking in Kingdom Authority

**Biblical Introduction: From Survival to Dominion**

God never intended for you to merely survive - He anointed you to reign. The first words spoken over mankind were not about worship - they were about dominion. *"Let them have dominion"* (Genesis 1:26). Before man was given a pulpit, he was given authority. Before he sang a song, he was told to subdue. Dominion is not arrogance - it is alignment. When you know who sent you, you stop apologizing for your presence.

You were never meant to ask permission from systems you were born to transform. The Kingdom is not a democracy - it is a government of glory, power, and order. You are not an ambassador of opinions - you are a carrier of authority. When you walk in Kingdom authority, you don't conform to atmospheres - you command them. You don't echo voices - you carry one. The voice of your King.

**Authority Is Not a Feeling**

Authority is not based on emotion - it's rooted in identity. You don't feel powerful to be powerful. You step into authority because it's your birthright in Christ. Jesus did not die to make you religious - He died to make you dangerous. Dangerous to darkness. Dangerous to bondage. Dangerous to Hell's hierarchy.

*"Behold, I give you authority..."* (Luke 10:19). Authority is not a concept. It's a weapon. And the Church has traded it for comfort. We've mistaken loudness for authority and passivity for humility. But Heaven is not looking for passive participants. It's summoning active sons.

When you understand authority, you speak differently. You pray differently. You walk into conflict with the knowledge that Heaven backs your voice. You don't negotiate with demons - you cast them out. You don't beg for victory - you enforce it (Mark 16:17).

The evidence of real authority is not volume - it's results. Demons don't flee because you yell louder; they flee because you're aligned. Real authority walks in boldness even when emotions are absent. It acts on truth, not impulse. You don't wait until you feel it. You release it because it's already yours (Ephesians 2:6).

**Authority Flows From Submission**

Authority does not exist apart from submission. Jesus Himself said, *"I only do what I see My Father do"* (John 5:19). Kingdom authority is not about control - it's about alignment. You cannot carry power unless you are under it.

Sons walk in authority because they stay under the voice of the Father. Rebels have noise. Sons have weight. Authority doesn't shout - it speaks and things move. Hell doesn't fear volume. It fears obedience.

The Centurion understood this: *"I also am a man under authority... say the word and my servant will be healed"* (Matthew 8:9). He recognized that authority works because of order. If you reject order, you forfeit impact. If you refuse to submit, you sabotage your seat.

Authority that does not flow from submission is fraudulent. It's theatrical but powerless. It may impress crowds, but it won't move Heaven. Submission anchors your authority in truth. It gives your words consequence. Without submission, authority is a costume.

Jesus proved His highest authority through His highest obedience. In Gethsemane, when He said, *"Not My will, but Yours be done,"* He positioned Himself to carry the cross - and all authority with it (Luke 22:42).

## Kingdom Authority Redefines Atmospheres

Wherever Jesus went, He redefined reality. Sickness fled. Storms bowed. Demons screamed. He didn't react to atmospheres - He ruled them. Because He walked in unshakable authority. *"What kind of man is this, that even the winds and the sea obey Him?"* (Matthew 8:27)

117

You were never designed to be a thermometer - you are a thermostat. You don't reflect your environment - you shift it. You don't echo your culture - you confront it. Kingdom authority means your presence becomes a verdict.

When you walk into a room, confusion should lose its grip. When you open your mouth, strongholds should begin to tremble. Why? Because you carry more than words - you carry weight. You carry a verdict from Heaven. You are not just anointed to sing, preach, or work. You are commissioned to take territory.

Kingdom authority carries the power to interrupt demonic momentum. It shifts atmospheres from chaos to clarity, from fear to faith, from anxiety to boldness. Your life becomes a climate, not a comment.

You're not there to accommodate dysfunction - you're there to displace it. You walk in with peace, and torment flees. You walk in with joy, and depression weakens. This is the kind of authority that rebuilds broken families, restores shattered identities, and brings life to dry bones (Ezekiel 37:4-5).

### The Authority of Voice

The enemy is not afraid of your silence. He is afraid of your voice. Because your voice carries the echo of your scroll. "Death and life are in the power of the tongue" (Proverbs 18:21).

Adam lost dominion when he went silent. Jesus restored it when He opened His mouth. *"It is written..."* (Matthew 4:4). The war was won by words. Your voice is a weapon. And silence is not humility - it's forfeiture.

Kingdom authority requires that you declare what God says, even when your surroundings disagree. You don't prophesy what you see - you prophesy what God said. You decree a thing, and it shall be established (Job 22:28).

The power of your voice is not in its tone - it's in its source. When your voice is rooted in the voice of the King, it carries governmental weight. It opens things. It shuts things. It binds. It looses (Matthew 18:18).

Your voice establishes jurisdiction. It's your divine right to evict what Heaven never planted. You are Heaven's ambassador. Your declarations carry legal weight in the spirit. The enemy understands legalities. He only resists what's unclear. But a decree from a seated son in authority cannot be ignored.

This is why you must stop speaking from frustration and start declaring from identity. Don't echo problems - prophesy solutions. Don't rehearse the enemy's lies - release Heaven's language (Isaiah 55:11).

## Authority Provokes Resistance

Don't expect to walk in authority and be left alone. The moment Jesus cast out demons, healed the sick, and flipped tables, resistance rose. Authority is a threat to every counterfeit system.

The early church didn't get persecuted for having services. They were targeted because they carried power. Power that disrupted economies. Power that exposed idols. Power that broke cycles. *"These who have turned the world upside down have come here also"* (Acts 17:6).

If your life doesn't provoke any opposition, you may not be walking in your full authority. Because true authority challenges comfort zones, disarms devils, and awakens dormant things. And Hell responds to that.

The moment authority manifests, control is threatened. Religious systems begin to riot. Political powers grow anxious. Familiar spirits become restless. Because when authority walks in, it rearranges everything.

Expect opposition, not because you did something wrong - but because you finally did something right. Resistance is often confirmation. You're no longer tolerated - you're a threat. Stand firm. Keep swinging. You're not fighting for authority - you're fighting from it (Ephesians 6:12-13).

## Kingdom Authority Is Heaven's Answer to Earth's Confusion

The earth is not in need of more celebrities. It groans for sons. It groans for those who carry weight - not clout. Power - not performance. The manifestation of the sons of God is the antidote to cultural chaos (Romans 8:19).

The rise of Kingdom authority in you will offend systems, but it will liberate cities. It will dismantle cycles. It will rebuild ruins. When authority is restored to its rightful place, identity follows, healing comes, and order returns.

You were born for more than influence - you were born for impact. Influence impresses people. Authority transforms nations. God is not asking you to fit in. He's commissioning you to stand out. To speak like Heaven. To walk like Christ. To rule as intended.

Heaven does not measure your life by how safe you played it - it measures your life by how much of the Kingdom you brought to Earth. You weren't saved to survive. You were saved to govern. You were called out to step in. Now is the time to rise as a son, speak as an ambassador, and rule as an heir (Romans 5:17).

## Conclusion: You Carry the Crown

You're not waiting on authority - you're walking in it. You're not a beggar at the gates. You're a son in the palace. You've been given keys. You've been given access. You've been given the Name above every name.

So rise up. Speak up. Step in. Hell doesn't get the last word - Heaven does. And Heaven has spoken over you: dominion, authority, and victory.

You are not powerless. You are not passive. You are not small. You carry the crown.

**Scripture Index:**

# Chapter Fourteen

## Advancing the Kingdom Through You

### Biblical Introduction: The Kingdom Advances Through the Obedient

Jesus didn't come merely to establish a religion - He came to inaugurate a Kingdom. One that would invade the earth not through force, but through surrendered vessels. *"Of the increase of His government and peace there shall be no end"* (Isaiah 9:7). This Kingdom does not retreat. It advances. And the question of Heaven is not, "Will God move?" but "Will you move with Him?"

You were not saved to spectate. You were rescued to rule. Not in arrogance, but in purpose. You are not a fan of the Kingdom - you are its expression. You are not waiting on revival. You are the revival. And when your identity aligns with Heaven's intent, the Kingdom begins to advance - through your hands, your words, your posture, your presence.

### You Are the Strategy

God's strategy to change the world isn't a program. It's a person.

You.

When God wants to shift a region, He sends a son. When Heaven wants to interrupt a system, it births a voice. The plan of God has always been incarnational. It's not just preached - it's embodied. *"The Kingdom of God is within you"* (Luke 17:21).

You are not waiting on the next wave - you are called to be the wave. You are not praying for movement - you are becoming movement. The Kingdom doesn't expand by accident. It expands when sons and daughters step into their assignment without apology.

This is why Hell fights your clarity. Because if you ever realize who you are, you become the threat. You stop living on defense and start taking territory. And the places the enemy once occupied become testimonies of divine reversal.

You don't need a massive audience to make a Kingdom impact - you just need obedience. God is still using one voice to confront armies, one life to flip cities, one surrendered vessel to make eternal ripples (Judges 6:12-16). You are not just the messenger - you are part of the message. Your life is a prophetic sign that God is not done with this generation.

### The Kingdom Doesn't Advance in Silence

The Kingdom of God suffers violence, and the violent take it by force (Matthew 11:12). Passivity has no place in a world at war. You are not called to survive darkness - you're called to overthrow it.

124

Silence is not peace - it's permission. What you tolerate, you authorize. And what you remain silent about, you surrender to. The Kingdom cannot advance through agreement with culture. It only advances through collision.

When Jesus preached the Kingdom, demons manifested. Religion shook. Politics raged. Why? Because the Kingdom never arrives unnoticed. It carries confrontation. And when it is proclaimed with purity and power, everything that is false begins to collapse.

You are not here to echo the crowd - you are here to declare the crown. Your words are not suggestions - they are decrees. Your prayers are not whispers - they are weapons. Your declarations do not flatter - they demolish strongholds (2 Corinthians 10:4-5).

Your silence is not humility - it's abdication. The Kingdom must be spoken. Power must be declared. Truth must be lifted above the noise. When you open your mouth with Heaven's language, strongholds shatter and demons scatter (Jeremiah 1:10).

This is not the time to blend in. This is the moment to roar. To prophesy in public what God has whispered in private. The Kingdom advances where the people of God declare without fear and live without compromise.

## Movement Requires Momentum

The Kingdom moves with momentum. But momentum requires motion. You cannot advance what you refuse to move in.

Many are waiting for clarity while Heaven is waiting for obedience.

*"Go into all the world..."* (Mark 16:15). The Kingdom is not waiting on a conference - it's waiting on your movement. It grows through steps of faith, not circles of confusion. The longer you delay, the more ground remains unclaimed.

If you wait until you're ready, you'll never move. But the Kingdom doesn't advance through perfection - it advances through obedience. When you go, grace meets you. When you speak, Heaven backs you. Movement is the language of dominion.

You won't always see the outcome. But obedience isn't about sight - it's about trust. Abraham didn't have a map, but he had a word (Hebrews 11:8). And that was enough to birth nations.

Momentum is built in the going. Every step of obedience multiplies impact. Every act of risk increases reach. The Kingdom is like leaven - it spreads when it is activated (Matthew 13:33). You are not just an observer of Kingdom growth - you are a catalyst.

Delay is disobedience disguised in logic. Waiting for the perfect moment is often fear wearing faith's vocabulary. But faith without movement is fiction. When you move, the Kingdom moves with you.

## The Kingdom Is Carried by Sons, Not Spectators

God is not building a fan club. He's establishing a family. A Kingdom of sons who carry their Father's business with weight and honor. You are not an employee of Heaven. You are an heir (Romans 8:17).

Sons don't wait for someone else to act. Sons move because they carry the DNA of the King. They carry responsibility, not excuses. They don't wait for the atmosphere to change - they release one.

Spectators celebrate events. Sons establish eras. You weren't saved to clap - you were commissioned to conquer. This is why God calls you a co-laborer, not a co-watcher (1 Corinthians 3:9).

When you step into your sonship, you stop chasing affirmation and start carrying assignment. Your identity becomes your weapon. Your obedience becomes your legacy. You don't need a stage. You need a scroll. And when you read it, you'll realize - it was always about territory.

Sons don't need approval - they walk in authority. They don't wait for votes - they stand on vision. Spectators observe what God is doing. Sons become what He is doing. You don't carry a moment - you carry a mantle.

When God finds a son, He establishes a movement. From Abraham to David to Jesus, history was shifted not by crowds but by consecrated carriers. And now, the torch is in your hands.

## Kingdom Advancement Is a Violent Reversal

Every place the Kingdom enters, something dies. Sin dies. Shame dies. Fear dies. The Kingdom doesn't ask for room - it takes it. It displaces what was there with what has always been written.

Your life becomes a battlefield of reversal. The curses that were spoken over your family? Reversed. The cycles that defined your past? Broken. The labels you believed? Destroyed. Because the Kingdom never enters to negotiate. It enters to dominate.

And that dominance doesn't look like control - it looks like transformation. You walk into a room, and peace replaces panic. You speak, and truth silences deception. You act, and cycles begin to unravel. This is the Holy violence of love. It overturns tables. It heals on the Sabbath. It raises what religion buried (Matthew 21:12-14).

You are not here to coexist with evil. You are here to crush it underfoot (Romans 16:20). The God of peace advances through sons of war.

The cross was Heaven's violent reversal. What looked like defeat became dominion. What looked like weakness released resurrection. And now, that same reversal power lives in you. You're not here to maintain the atmosphere - you are here to tear it down and rebuild it with glory (2 Corinthians 10:5).

## The Kingdom Is Not Just Coming - It Has Come

Jesus did not say the Kingdom is coming someday. He said, *"The Kingdom of Heaven is at hand"* (Matthew 4:17). The

Kingdom is not distant - it is present. It is not theoretical - it is tangible. And you are the proof.

Everywhere your feet step, the Kingdom steps. Every conversation you carry, the Kingdom speaks. Every act of obedience you take, the Kingdom moves. You don't have to manufacture a move of God - you are the move.

You are not hosting revival - you are revival. You are not waiting on the Spirit - you walk with Him. The same Spirit that raised Christ from the dead lives in you (Romans 8:11). That means resurrection is not just your history - it's your authority.

Don't wait for the atmosphere to change - become the shift. Don't wait for permission - carry the commission. Don't ask when the Kingdom will come - announce that it already has.

The Kingdom is not waiting for perfect people - it's moving through available ones. The harvest isn't postponed - it's ready (John 4:35). All that's missing is laborers who understand: the Kingdom doesn't move through talent, it moves through trust.

You don't need to qualify yourself. The cross already did. You don't need to ask Heaven to show up - it already did. Now, carry it. Reveal it. Walk it out with boldness. The Kingdom has come, and you are its evidence.

## Conclusion: The King Advances Through You

The increase of His government is not up for debate - it's inevitable. The only question is whether you will participate. The

Kingdom is moving. Glory is rising. Sons are awakening. And Hell is trembling.

You are not powerless. You are not hidden. You are not waiting.

You are the advance.

## Scripture Index:

# Chapter Fifteen

## The Dangerous Prayer That Changes Everything

### Biblical Introduction: The Prayer That Heaven Answers

Some prayers move you. But there are some that move Heaven - and shake Hell. Not all prayers are safe. Not all prayers are polite. Some prayers carry fire in their bones and weight in their words. These are not prayers for comfort - they are calls to transformation. They don't negotiate - they surrender. They don't ask for protection - they beg for purpose. And when they are prayed, the atmosphere shifts.

God is not obligated to answer prayers that protect your comfort. But He rushes to respond when your words align with your scroll. The dangerous prayer is this: *"Here I am. Send me."* (Isaiah 6:8). It is not poetic. It is prophetic. It will break you, build you, and reintroduce you to the version of yourself Heaven wrote.

### The Death of the Safe Life

The safe life is the counterfeit gospel. It is the anesthetized version of discipleship, where Jesus becomes your therapist and not your Lord. The dangerous prayer dismantles that illusion. When you say, "Send me," you are volunteering for fire. You are inviting the cross to shape you and the Spirit to move through you.

The Kingdom never advanced through the comfortable. It has always moved through the surrendered. The ones who didn't count the cost because they already counted themselves dead. The ones who weren't trying to fit in - but trying to flame out for the glory of God.

God never called you to survive Babylon. He called you to confront it. And that confrontation begins with a whisper: "Send me." That whisper unleashes a war. Not outside - but inside. Because before God sends you out, He burns everything in you that would sabotage the assignment.

A safe life never produces supernatural fruit. It pacifies the soul but paralyzes the spirit. A safe life teaches you to manage your calling rather than embody it. But those who cry "Send me" are asking to be poured out like a drink offering (Philippians 2:17). They no longer crave preservation - they crave purpose.

## The Sifting Before the Sending

Before God sends a man or woman, He breaks them. Not to destroy - but to prepare. The dangerous prayer activates a dangerous process. One that will not spare your pride. One that will not coddle your excuses. God does not anoint potential. He anoints surrender.

When you say, "Send me," God begins to separate you. From distractions. From distortions. From dependency on people. Your circle may shrink, but your capacity expands. Because those who are truly sent don't live off applause - they live off obedience.

The sifting doesn't mean rejection - it means preparation. Joseph was sent through a pit. Moses was sent through exile. David was sent through caves. Jesus was sent through Gethsemane. The dangerous prayer enrolls you in Heaven's curriculum of transformation. And the diploma is not a platform - it's fire in your bones.

In the sifting, God burns out mixture. He tears away the layers that sought affirmation from people instead of His presence. You no longer serve for reward - you serve for obedience. You don't strive for opportunity - you steward responsibility. You are trained in private so that your authority in public is unshakable.

## A Voice That Cannot Be Silenced

The dangerous prayer awakens a voice. Not just a speaking voice - but a spiritual roar. You were never meant to be silent. You were never meant to whisper your assignment. The prayer "Send me" unlocks a voice that becomes thunder in dry places.

You do not echo culture - you confront it. You don't conform - you prophesy. Your voice becomes a sword that pierces the atmosphere. Not because of volume, but because of authority. The one who has been sent carries the weight of the throne.

133

Jeremiah said, *"His word is like a fire shut up in my bones"* (Jeremiah 20:9). When you pray the dangerous prayer, the Word of the Lord begins to possess you. You no longer read the Word - you release it. And that release causes rebellion to tremble, religion to scatter, and the hungry to run to the flame.

This voice carries a tone not birthed in training but in encounter. Your words break demonic agreements. Your decrees carry legal weight in the spirit. You become an oracle, not just a student. You don't echo sermons - you echo Heaven. And that sound cannot be silenced.

### You Will Lose Your Life

The dangerous prayer is not prayed by those who want to be safe - it's prayed by those who want to be consumed. When Isaiah said, "Send me," he was not applying for a job. He was laying his life on the altar. The prayer is an invitation to death. Not physical - but ego, agenda, and applause.

You don't get to carry this mantle and keep your image. The anointing will expose you. It will offend the systems you once tried to please. You will lose followers. You will lose invitations. But you will gain sight. You will gain presence. You will gain glory.

Jesus said, *"Whoever loses his life for My sake will find it"* (Matthew 16:25). The dangerous prayer empties you. But in that emptiness, God fills you with authority. Your life is no longer your own. You become a scroll, walking.

The real danger is not praying the prayer - it's refusing to. For in holding on to your life, you lose it (Luke 9:24). But in laying it down, you discover that what God gives back is not survival - it's resurrection. You become a living altar, a vessel of divine interruption.

## Assignment Over Agreement

Those who pray the dangerous prayer don't need consensus. They need confirmation. Heaven does not vote on your calling. God doesn't take polls before He sends. The ones who are truly sent carry something that requires no explanation - they just obey.

Assignment will always offend those in agreement with culture. But you weren't called to blend in. You were called to break through. You were sent as a sign, not a suggestion. Your life is not an option - it is a mandate. And when you walk in that authority, systems shift.

You may be misunderstood. You may be maligned. But Heaven is watching. And Hell is trembling. Because when a sent one enters the room, chains start to break. Not because of charisma - but because of consecration.

Agreement creates cliques. Assignment births movements. You don't gather to be liked - you gather to be launched. Your approval rating in Heaven is not tied to public applause. It's tied to your yes in secret. You choose alignment over applause. You embrace the wilderness over the crowd. Because sent ones walk with fire, not favor.

## Fire in Your Bones

The dangerous prayer does not produce religious activity - it births Holy fire. You cannot pray "Send me" and stay casual. You cannot be lit by the throne and still crave the stage. Those who are sent burn. And their burn becomes a beacon.

You won't need to market yourself - your flame will find the assignment. God sets fire to those He sends. Because what you carry is not information - it's impartation. What you bring is not strategy - it's surrender.

Elijah was a man sent by fire (2 Kings 1:10). The disciples were marked by fire (Acts 2:3). The early church advanced by fire. And now, the fire is falling again. But it only lands on the laid-down ones. The ones who prayed, "Here I am."

Holy fire is  Heaven's stamp of authenticity. The ones who burn without burnout are those consumed by purpose, not applause. You live like a torch. Every room you enter becomes an altar. You are not merely influential - you are incendiary.

## Hell Recognizes the Sent

When you've been sent, Hell knows your name. The seven sons of Sceva tried to imitate power, and the demons replied, *"Jesus I know, and Paul I know, but who are you?"* (Acts 19:15). Hell doesn't fear titles - it fears evidence. And evidence comes from being sent.

You don't scare the enemy by quoting sermons. You terrify him when you carry scars. The dangerous prayer makes you recognizable in the realm of the spirit. You stop being a churchgoer - you become a carrier of glory.

Your name is registered in two realms - Heaven and Hell. Heaven marks you as trusted. Hell marks you as targeted. And in that tension, you rise. Because you are not afraid. You have already died. The prayer has changed everything.

Hell marks those who carry weight. You are no longer tolerated - you are tracked. You are no longer overlooked - you are opposed. Because sent ones disrupt systems. They rattle thrones. They displace darkness. The moment you pray that prayer, your name is known in regions beyond.

## Conclusion: Pray It Anyway

You've heard the cost. You've seen the fire. And now the decision is yours. Will you pray the dangerous prayer? Will you surrender the safe life? Will you become the scroll that walks, the flame that speaks, the voice that breaks chains?

He is still asking, "Whom shall I send, and who will go for us?" And somewhere inside you, something is burning to respond.

Say it. "Here I am. Send me."

## Scripture Index:

# Chapter Sixteen

## The Emergence of the Anomaly

### Why the World Needs Holy Disruptors

The days of passive Christianity are over. The earth is
groaning under the weight of its rebellion, and creation itself waits
in anticipation for the revealing of the sons of God (Romans 8:19).
Systems are collapsing, governments are faltering, morality is
dissolving, and truth has been traded for opinion. In such an hour,
Heaven does not simply send comforters - it sends catalysts. The
Kingdom births a breed of believers who cannot be bought,
cannot be bribed, and cannot be broken. These are the Holy
disruptors.

A Holy disruptor is not a reckless troublemaker but a
divine instrument of confrontation. They do not tear down for the
sake of destruction - they confront in order to rebuild according to
Heaven's blueprint. Where culture resigns itself to, "This is just
how it is," the disruptor declares, "Thus says the Lord - prepare
the way for the King." They walk into the epicenters of
compromise carrying an atmosphere that demands decision.

They are necessary because the world has settled into a
counterfeit peace. The prophet Jeremiah warned against this when
he said, *"They have healed the wound of my people lightly, saying, 'Peace,*

*peace,' when there is no peace"* (Jeremiah 6:14). Disruptors refuse to apply soothing words to mortal wounds - they will not tell a generation drowning in sin that they are fine as they are. They bring the kind of truth that shakes people from their slumber.

If the culture can't tell you've arrived, you're not carrying the Kingdom. Revival doesn't come to the comfortable - it comes to the desperate who disrupt the darkness.

Without Holy disruptors, the Church becomes a mirror of the culture instead of the mold of the Kingdom. Jesus described His disciples as salt and light (Matthew 5:13-16) - two agents that change whatever they touch. Salt preserves and stings at the same time; light exposes even as it illuminates. Disruptors are both. They irritate complacency and illuminate destiny.

They are the divine answer to the dangerous comfort of religion without power (Mark 7:13). They will not allow God's people to hide behind tradition or empty ritual. Like Jesus overturning tables in the temple (Matthew 21:12-13), they confront the misuse of sacred space and restore it to its intended glory.

The Church without disruptors becomes stagnant, like a body of water with no outflow. But the Church with disruptors becomes a rushing river, unstoppable and life-giving. These are Heaven's prophetic demolition crews, tearing down strongholds of thought (2 Corinthians 10:4-5) so new foundations of truth can be laid.

## The Anointing of the Uncommon

Every anomaly in the Kingdom carries something that can't be imitated or mass-produced - an anointing that marks them as Heaven's property. This is not a personality trait, a leadership skill, or the fruit of clever branding. It is the residue of divine encounter. *"But you have been anointed by the Holy One, and you all have knowledge"* (1 John 2:20).

"Your anointing will make you look strange to those who have learned to live without power."

"You're not supposed to fit in; you're supposed to stand out until standing out becomes the new normal."

The uncommon anointing makes its carrier stand out, even in a crowd of the anointed. David walked into a battlefield full of soldiers, but he was the only one who saw Goliath through the lens of covenant with God (1 Samuel 17:26, 1 Samuel 17:32). This is what the anointing does - it doesn't just make you bold, it makes you perceive reality from Heaven's vantage point.

Uncommon anointing is never given without separation. Moses did not receive his call while seated in Pharaoh's palace but in the obscurity of the wilderness. Joseph's dreams were not fulfilled in the comfort of his father's tent but through the crucible of betrayal, false accusation, and prison. Separation sanctifies the carrier so that the anointing flows pure and undiluted.

Those with uncommon anointing disrupt atmospheres simply by entering them. They carry the fragrance of Heaven's throne room into earthly spaces (2 Corinthians 2:14-15). They expose the counterfeit not by argument but by authenticity - light doesn't have to debate darkness to prove it's light; it simply shines.

And because it is uncommon, it must be guarded. Samson was anointed to begin delivering Israel from the Philistines (Judges 13:5), but compromise drained his strength. The anomaly must learn from this - your distinction is not negotiable. The moment you try to make your anointing "acceptable" to the world, you disarm it.

## You Were Not Sent to Blend In - You Were Sent to Ignite

Blending in is the slow suffocation of your assignment. Jesus warned that salt which loses its saltiness is worthless (Matthew 5:13). The anomaly understands this - when you start to sound like everyone else, you cease to be effective.

If your presence doesn't shift the atmosphere, your absence won't be noticed. You're not the match in God's hand to warm the room - you're the torch to set it ablaze.

You were not sent to be background noise in the symphony of culture. You were sent as a firebrand. John the Baptist did not emerge from the wilderness whispering polite encouragements; he thundered a call to repentance that shook cities. Fire attracts both the desperate and the dangerous - it comforts the cold and provokes the resistant.

Igniting a culture requires friction. To spark anything, there must be resistance. Paul ignited riots and revivals in equal measure (Acts 17:6). Everywhere he went, things shifted. Idols were overturned. Economic systems tied to darkness collapsed. Demons were cast out. The environment could not remain neutral once the Kingdom arrived.

To ignite is to risk rejection. Fire consumes, and not everyone wants their comfort burned away. Jesus Himself said, *"Do you think I came to bring peace on earth? No, I tell you, but division"* (Luke 12:51). This is not division for ego's sake - it is the separation of truth from deception, light from darkness.

If you were sent to ignite, you must accept the reality that your presence will disrupt people's carefully constructed illusions. You will provoke questions they don't want to ask and expose answers they'd rather ignore. And that is exactly why you cannot blend in - you carry the match Heaven intends to strike.


## The Rise of the Elijah Generation

The Elijah generation is here - a remnant that refuses to bow to the idols of culture or the counterfeits in the Church. Elijah stood before King Ahab and declared a drought without flinching (1 Kings 17:1). His courage was not born from arrogance but from standing in the presence of God before standing before men.

Elijah didn't wait for consensus; he called down fire until consensus bowed to truth. The remnant is rising - not to echo culture, but to confront it.

This generation will walk in that same boldness. They will confront not just the prophets of Baal but the compromises within the camp of God's people. They will repair altars before calling down fire (1 Kings 18:30-39), knowing that public power flows from private consecration.

They are confrontational by assignment. Like Elijah, they will stand on Mount Carmel, outnumbered yet unshaken. They will defy the mob, not because they enjoy the fight, but because they know that the fear of man produces compromise, and compromise quenches revival.

The Elijah generation will also be restorers. They will not just call down fire but rebuild what was broken. They will reestablish holiness where it has been mocked, truth where it has been silenced, and worship where it has been replaced by performance.

And they will overcome the spirit of Jezebel - a demonic force of intimidation, manipulation, and silencing - that seeks to neutralize prophetic voices (Revelation 2:20). But like Elijah's mantle that fell on Elisha, this generation's courage will outlive their critics.

## You Are Not the Alternative - You Are the Assignment

Heaven did not send you as one option among many - it sent you as the answer. Paul told the Galatians he was *"an apostle - sent not from men nor by man, but by Jesus Christ"* (Galatians 1:1). That kind of clarity kills insecurity.

God didn't send you as a suggestion; He sent you as the solution. When you understand you are the assignment, you stop auditioning for approval.

You are not a substitute teacher filling in until someone better comes along. You are the one chosen for the specific people, place, and time to which you have been sent. The unique DNA of your calling is the exact combination required for your assignment.

When you realize you are the assignment, you stop trying to imitate others. You stop competing for platforms that are not yours. You stop apologizing for your authority. You understand that you are not called to fit someone else's mold - you are called to break it.

And with that realization comes weight. Being the assignment is not about comfort; it is about responsibility. Jeremiah tried to protest his call, but God silenced his excuses with, *"Before I formed you in the womb I knew you, before you were born I set you apart"* (Jeremiah 1:5). If you are set apart, you cannot live like you are common.

### "This Is That": Becoming Heaven's Fulfillment

When Peter declared on Pentecost, *"This is that which was spoken by the prophet Joel"* (Acts 2:16), he was standing in a prophetic fulfillment that had been centuries in the making. He was living proof that God's word does not return void (Isaiah 55:11).

"Prophecy was never meant to stay on paper - it was meant to walk in your shoes."

When Heaven says 'This is that,' earth has no choice but to shift.

To become a "this is that" vessel means your life becomes the living evidence that God keeps His promises. You stop talking about what God *might* do and start manifesting what He *is* doing.

These moments happen when preparation meets prophecy. They are not confined to revival meetings - they erupt in boardrooms, classrooms, neighborhoods, and nations. The "this is that" vessel carries a readiness to move when Heaven speaks, knowing that delayed obedience is disobedience.

Living this way requires faith that does not demand all the details. Mary, the mother of Jesus, became a "this is that" fulfillment of Isaiah's prophecy simply by saying, *"Let it be to me according to your word"* (Luke 1:38).

Your assignment is not random - it is a prophetic thread woven into the story God has been writing since before you were born. To live as a "this is that" vessel is to embrace the privilege and pressure of being the visible proof that Heaven's decrees have invaded earth.

## Scripture Index:

- Romans 8:19
- Jeremiah 6:14
- Matthew 5:13-16
- Mark 7:13
- Matthew 21:12-13
- 2 Corinthians 10:4-5
- 1 John 2:20
- 1 Samuel 17:26
- 1 Samuel 17:32
- 2 Corinthians 2:14-15
- Judges 13:5
- Acts 17:6
- Luke 12:51
- 1 Kings 17:1
- 1 Kings 18:30-39
- Revelation 2:20
- Galatians 1:1
- Jeremiah 1:5
- Acts 2:16
- Isaiah 55:11
- Luke 1:38

# Chapter Seventeen

## Breaking the Spirit of the Herd

### The Danger of Cloning in the Church

The Kingdom was never designed to operate on mass-produced replicas. Heaven is a master artisan, not a factory foreman. God did not put His image in man so that we could spend our lives mimicking other men. Yet, in the modern church, there is a creeping epidemic of cloning - leaders copying leaders, churches duplicating other churches, and believers wearing another person's mantle instead of their own.

"When you blend in, you lose the authority to call anyone out. The herd celebrates safety; the Kingdom rewards obedience. When you conform to the mold, you disqualify yourself from breaking it.

The herd spirit thrives on the illusion of unity through sameness. It mistakes uniformity for spiritual maturity, and imitation for inspiration. But God never blesses what He did not birth. Saul's armor may have been respectable, but David's sling was effective (1 Samuel 17:38-40).

Israel was commanded to remain distinct from the surrounding nations (Leviticus 20:26). They were never meant to blend with the customs, values, and idols of the people around them. The herd spirit whispers, "Be like them and they will like you." The Spirit of God declares, "Be like Me and I will be with you."

The danger of cloning is not simply that it robs you of identity - it robs the world of the unique facet of God's image you were meant to reveal. When the church functions as a herd, it may move together, but it moves in circles, never advancing into new territory.

"Cloning creates carbon copies, but the Kingdom calls for original blueprints."

## God's Voice vs. Group Consensus

The herd instinct bows to the majority. If enough people agree, it must be true - or so the herd thinks. But truth is not subject to popular vote. God's voice is not a democracy - it is a decree.

God's voice will often contradict group consensus - learn to choose Him over them. Agreement with Heaven will often look like rebellion on earth. The voice of the many can drown out the whisper of God - unless you choose silence before Him.

At Kadesh Barnea, twelve spies were sent into the Promised Land. Ten returned with fear, two with faith (Numbers 13:31-33). The herd went with the ten, and an entire generation died wandering in the wilderness. Joshua and Caleb stood with the minority, not because they enjoyed isolation, but because they recognized the difference between sight and revelation.

The crowd will choose safety over sacrifice every time. It will shout "Hosanna!" on Sunday and "Crucify Him!" on Friday. This is why those who follow the crowd will never finish the race God has marked out for them.

Noah built an ark without the backing of public opinion. Abraham left his homeland without knowing his destination. The apostles stood before the Sanhedrin and declared, *"We must obey God rather than men"* (Acts 5:29).

If the crowd approves your calling, it's probably not from Heaven.

The herd instinct must be broken in the secret place. Only there can you learn to value His voice over the roar of the masses.

## Standing Alone Before Leading Many

Kingdom leadership does not begin when people follow you - it begins when you obey God alone. The ability to stand alone is the foundation for leading with authority.

If you can't stand alone, you're not ready to lead many. It's better to walk alone with God than with a crowd going nowhere. Isolation with God is preparation for influence with man.

Moses confronted Pharaoh without a support team. Elijah faced the prophets of Baal alone (1 Kings 18:19-40). Jesus stood before Pilate while His disciples scattered.

The herd will only follow you when it is safe, convenient, or beneficial. But leaders forged in the fires of solitude follow God whether anyone else comes with them or not.

Standing alone purifies motives. If your obedience depends on applause, you will quit the moment criticism comes. God allows seasons of aloneness to teach you that your strength comes from His presence, not people's approval.

If standing for truth leaves you standing alone, you are still in the majority with God.

## When the Model Becomes the Idol

God may give you a model to follow, but He never intends the model to replace His voice. The herd instinct clings to familiar systems even after God has moved on.

When the model becomes the idol, it's time to break the mold. Crowds chase signs; sons carry them.

The bronze serpent was once God's instrument for healing (Numbers 21:8-9). Centuries later, Israel began to worship it as an idol until King Hezekiah destroyed it (2 Kings 18:4). What was once a tool from God became a stumbling block to His people.

The herd often mistakes method for anointing. It builds monuments to yesterday's moves of God, unaware that the cloud has moved on. Models should serve the mission, but when the mission starts serving the model, the Spirit is grieved.

151

When the model outlives the movement, it becomes a monument.

True reformers know when to honor the past without being bound to it. They refuse to worship the tools God used and instead remain committed to the God who used them.

### Distinction Is the Mark of Divine Favor

In the herd, everyone looks the same, talks the same, acts the same. But in the Kingdom, distinction is proof of divine favor.

Distinction isn't arrogance - it's stewardship of divine favor. Favor will make you a target before it makes you a testimony.

Joseph's multicolored coat set him apart in his father's house, but it also made him a target for his brothers' jealousy (Genesis 37:3-4). Daniel's refusal to defile himself in Babylon distinguished him and drew both favor from the king and hatred from his rivals (Daniel 1:8-9).

Distinction is costly. It will open doors in palaces and dungeons alike. Those who crave the safety of the herd will never walk in the weight of favor, because favor magnifies you - and magnified people are easier to attack.

If your favor doesn't frighten the insecure, it probably isn't from God.

The point of favor is not your elevation but God's demonstration. You are set apart so that the world can see His goodness through you.

## Kill the Herd Instinct - Follow the Cloud

The herd instinct will keep you where it's comfortable if the presence of God has moved on. Israel was guided by the cloud by day and the pillar of fire by night. When the cloud moved, they moved (Numbers 9:17-23). If they stayed when God moved, they were left behind.

If the cloud moves and the crowd doesn't, follow the cloud. You can't follow the cloud and the crowd at the same time. The herd will keep you safe; the cloud will keep you alive.

The cloud represents the unpredictable leading of the Holy Spirit. It will take you out of predictable patterns and into territory where only trust sustains you. Those who stay with the crowd may feel safe, but they are stuck. Those who follow the cloud may feel stretched, but they are alive in the will of God.

"It's better to walk into the unknown with God than to sit in the familiar without Him."

Following the cloud requires an untethered heart. It demands that you value presence over popularity and obedience over optics. The herd will mock you for leaving, but the glory will rest on those who move with God.

**Scripture Index:**

- Leviticus 20:26
- 1 Samuel 17:38-40
- Numbers 13:31-33
- Acts 5:29
- 1 Kings 18:19-40
- Numbers 21:8-9
- 2 Kings 18:4
- Genesis 37:3-4
- Daniel 1:8-9
- Numbers 9:17-23

# Chapter Eighteen

## The Generation That Finishes the Scroll

### The Scroll Is Open - Now Walk It

The seals are broken, and Heaven's scroll is no longer sealed in mystery. Revelation has shifted from hidden to revealed, from prophecy to pathway. The generation that finishes the scroll must not only read it - they must walk it out in flesh and blood. This is a summons to incarnation, where what was once only vision in the Spirit becomes reality in the earth. *"Blessed is the one who reads aloud the words of this prophecy, and blessed are those who hear, and who keep what is written in it"* (Revelation 1:3).

To walk the scroll is to make the unseen visible. "What Heaven releases must find earthly expression, or it dies as a concept instead of becoming a conquest." It means confronting injustice with righteousness (Isaiah 1:17), answering chaos with divine order (1 Corinthians 14:33), and replacing hopelessness with the promises of God (Romans 15:13). This generation will understand that obedience to the scroll is not seasonal - it is a lifelong march (Hebrews 12:1-2). They will carry Kingdom decrees into every sphere of society, manifesting divine authority in places where compromise once ruled. Like John the Baptist, they will prepare the way (Isaiah 40:3) with uncompromising truth, their lives marked by courage, sacrifice, and unwavering loyalty to the King.

## Prophetic Identity Must Become Tangible Assignment

It is not enough to know who you are prophetically; the question is, what will you do with that identity? Heaven's declarations are blueprints, not trophies. Like Jeremiah, the

word must be fire in your bones until it is released into action (Jeremiah 20:9). "Identity celebrated without assignment executed is deception disguised as destiny."

Identity proves itself through obedience (John 14:15). When Jesus called His disciples, He not only named them - He sent them (John 20:21). Tangible assignment turns revelation into action. Faith without works is dead (James 2:17), and light hidden under a basket changes nothing (Matthew 5:14-16). This generation will turn prophetic identity into measurable Kingdom influence: planting churches (Acts 14:23), shifting atmospheres (Acts 16:25-26), restoring broken systems (Nehemiah 2:17-18), and releasing strategies from Heaven (Proverbs 21:22). Heaven measures your calling not by how well you understand it, but by how fully you fulfill it.

## The Mantle Must Be Multiplied, Not Memorialized

The temptation of every move of God is to turn a living mantle into a museum artifact. But the anointing was never meant to be preserved - it was meant to be poured out. Elisha asked for a double portion because he understood mantles are for multiplication (2 Kings 2:9-14).

If the mantle stops with you, the mission dies with you. The finishing generation will see mantles as rivers designed to overflow into others (John 7:38). Jesus promised greater works for those who believe (John 14:12). This requires intentional discipleship (2 Timothy 2:2), the deliberate transfer of wisdom (Proverbs 13:20), anointing (Isaiah 61:1), and authority (Luke 10:19). Mantles will not be locked away in legacies - they will be multiplied in sons and daughters who will carry them further, faster, and into territories yet unreached.

## The Last Shall Be First: Final Hour Workers

Jesus spoke of laborers entering the vineyard at the final hour and receiving the same reward as those who had worked all day (Matthew 20:1-16). Hidden in obscurity until the final trumpet of assignment, they emerge with the speed of Heaven's urgency.

These last-hour workers will be marked by a fierce focus (Philippians 3:13-14). Like the thief on the cross who entered Paradise in his final hour (Luke 23:42-43), their window of influence may be short, but their obedience will carry eternal weight (2 Corinthians 4:17). God is redeeming time (Joel 2:25), collapsing years into moments, and releasing harvesters who will accomplish in months what others could not in decades (Amos

9:13). Their presence will shake the complacent (Ephesians 5:14) and inspire the faithful to finish their race with endurance (Hebrews 12:1).

**Sons of Issachar: Understanding Times and Seasons**

1 Chronicles 12:32 speaks of the sons of Issachar, men who understood the times and knew what Israel should do. They are Heaven's strategists - prophetic timekeepers ensuring the Church arrives on Heaven's schedule.

In a generation flooded with opinions, these discerners will be a compass for the Body of Christ (Proverbs 4:7). They will read the signs (Matthew 16:3), interpret the shifts (Daniel 2:21), and position God's people for decisive moments. Without their guidance, the Church risks acting too soon or too late; with it, she moves in perfect step with Heaven's calendar (Ecclesiastes 3:1). They will train others to recognize kairos moments, to respond instantly when God moves (Isaiah 30:21), and to hold steady when He says wait (Habakkuk 2:3; Matthew 25:1-13).

**Finishing What the Fathers Saw**

The scroll contains visions and promises entrusted to fathers and mothers of the faith who did not see their fulfillment. Hebrews 11:39-40 says they did not receive the promise because God's plan included us.

Do not abandon the plow you inherited; finish the furrow they started. Like Joshua leading Israel into the Promised Land (Joshua 21:43-45), this generation will pick up where others left off. "The end of their vision is the beginning of your assignment." They will research (Proverbs 25:2), restore (Isaiah 58:12), and run with mandates that history tried to bury (Hebrews 12:1-2), carrying them to completion (Habakkuk 2:3). Their victories will validate the sacrifices of generations before them, and the sound of completion will echo through eternity (Revelation 7:9-10).

## Conclusion

The generation that finishes the scroll is marked by urgency, clarity, and unstoppable obedience. They will not rest in revelation alone - they will walk it out. They will turn identity into assignment, mantles into multiplication, discernment into timely action, and unfinished promises into fulfilled history. The scroll is open - now is the time to finish it.

## Scripture Index:

- Revelation 1:3
- Isaiah 40:3
- Isaiah 1:17
- 1 Corinthians 14:33
- Romans 15:13
- Hebrews 12:1-2

- John 14:15
- John 20:21
- James 2:17
- Matthew 5:14-16
- Acts 14:23
- Acts 16:25-26

- Nehemiah 2:17-18
- Proverbs 21:22
- 2 Kings 2:9-14
- John 7:38
- John 14:12
- 2 Timothy 2:2
- Proverbs 13:20
- Isaiah 61:1
- Luke 10:19
- Matthew 20:1-16
- Philippians 3:13-14
- Luke 23:42-43
- 2 Corinthians 4:17
- Joel 2:25
- Amos 9:13
- Ephesians 5:14
- 1 Chronicles 12:32
- Proverbs 4:7
- Matthew 16:3
- Daniel 2:21
- Ecclesiastes 3:1
- Isaiah 30:21
- Habakkuk 2:3
- Matthew 25:1-13
- Joshua 21:43-45
- Proverbs 25:2
- Isaiah 58:12
- Revelation 7:9-10

# Conclusion

## The Final Confrontation of Calling

You were not created for mediocrity. You were not formed to mimic the herd. You were designed by the hand of God with gifts, desires, and a fire that make you functional for daily life and essential for the Kingdom (Ephesians 2:10). But beyond function lies calling. Beyond calling lies the high calling—that place where the Spirit of God breathes hyperbolē into your nature, giving you the power to go further than flesh can carry you (2 Corinthians 4:7).

The high calling is not imagination. It is the anointing of God resting on design. Others may throw rocks, but when you throw, it sails beyond their reach. That is hyperbolē—your divine distinction. That is where the anointing falls. That is where Heaven verifies that you are not average, not forgotten, not wasted. You were born for this.

But hear me clearly: the anointing is not unconditional. The gifts of God may be irrevocable (Romans 11:29), but the anointing can be forfeited. Samson was born with promise, set apart from birth (Judges 13:5). Yet he despised his daily assignment, broke his vows, and surrendered his consecration to lust. The Spirit left him, and he *"did not know that the LORD had departed from him"* (Judges

16:20). Samson still had gifts, but the anointing was gone. He died chained and humiliated in the temple of a foreign god with his eyes poked out. He missed living in the high calling for his life, which was to be a **Deliverer.**

Contrast this with Samuel. As a boy, he served faithfully in the house of God (1 Samuel 3:1). He stewarded his daily assignment, but he also leaned in when Heaven whispered his name. Samuel became both judge and reached his high calling of a **Prophet**—a man who carried authority until the day of his death (1 Samuel 3:20; 1 Samuel 7:15). The difference? He cherished the call, stewarded the assignment, and never confused gifts with anointing.

Leaders, hear the word of the Lord: it is your sacred duty to father the emerging gifts in your house, creating the atmosphere to build them. Your task is not to suppress the hyperbolē in others, nor to manipulate it for your own gain. You are to create an atmosphere where gifts emerge and fruits are tested, not strangled. If you refuse, the people assigned to your mantle will become spiritual orphans. They will drift into the arms of other fathers because you were too insecure to release them. And their absence will testify against you when your own hands tremble with emptiness.

Because one day, you will step onto a platform to lay your hands on the people. And in that moment, the truth will be revealed. Nothing will happen. No power. No fire. The oil will be gone. What once surged like lightning will feel like silence. You will look at your own hands, shaking in fear, and whisper a desperate prayer: Please, Lord, let something happen this time. But if you did not repent before, if you did not father sons and daughters when God commanded, you will find yourself exposed. What you lost in private will be revealed in public just like Samson and Saul. The anointing does not answer to reputation—it answers to relationship.

Samuel walked in the high calling throughout his life. He stood as a **Prophet** who not only carried God's word but witnessed the power of that word shaping a nation. He lived to see the fruit of the anointing upon him and rejoiced in it.

Samson, however, squandered much of his journey. His high calling as a **Deliverer** only manifested in his final breath. He fulfilled it, but he never lived to see it—because it crushed him in the moment of his death.

Yet even here, hope remains. The story of Samson does not end in humiliation—it ends in restoration. Chained between pillars, blinded by sin and compromise, Samson prayed: *"O Lord God, remember me, I pray! Strengthen me, I pray, just this once"* (Judges 16:28). And the Lord answered. His hair had begun to grow again, and with one final act of surrender, Samson accomplished more in death than in all his life. Restoration came not by strength, but by repentance.

So it will be with you. Leader, pastor, prophet—if you repent, if you renounce the idol of "my ministry," if you confess that it was always God's Kingdom and God's glory, the fire will return. The "my ministry" spirit is not the Holy Spirit—it is an unclean spirit of pride and ownership, and it will strip you of power every time. The Holy Spirit only moves where Jesus is exalted, not where egos are enthroned. *"I am the LORD; that is my name! I will not give my glory to another, nor my praise to idols"* (Isaiah 42:8).

Pastor, if you're having problems getting the gifts flowing again in your life and in the body of the congregation you are stewarding—and if there is anyone still left in the body you're leading who is still on fire for God—find them. They are watching and waiting to have a relationship with you, and they will help get your fire back. In fact, it may be their assignment. That is what mature sons and daughters do: they support the whole family when they are mature.

Do not carry the counterfeit. Repent, and then get close to those who are burning. Fire is transferable. If you stand among the truly consecrated, if you humble yourself beside those who are ablaze with God's Spirit, that fire will ignite you again. *"Iron sharpens iron, and one man sharpens another"* (Proverbs 27:17). *"Fan into flame the gift of God, which is in you"* (2 Timothy 1:6). When you honor the fire in others, the Lord will rekindle it in you.

164

This is not about your brand. This is not about your reputation. This is not about your platform. It is about His glory. Always His glory. *"For from Him and through Him and to Him are all things. To Him be glory forever. Amen"* (Romans 11:36).

Do not wait until the anointing has lifted to repent. Do not become like Saul, who once carried oil but ended tormented by an evil spirit, abandoned by the voice of God (1 Samuel 16:14), caused by jealousy and pride. Do not cover your lack of power by silencing the gifted around you. Repent now. Raise sons and daughters now. Cry out, like Samson in his final hour, and the Lord will restore you.

The Kingdom does not need more performers. It needs fathers who release sons, prophets who train voices, and leaders who guard the flame of authenticity. The Spirit is saying to the Church: Awaken, align, and arise. The hour is late, but the assignment is still alive.

Do not bury your scroll. Do not waste your days in borrowed armor. Do not echo when you were called to roar. Heaven has already written your book (Psalm 40:7–8; Hebrews 10:7). One day, the Judge of all will compare what you lived with what He wrote (Revelation 20:12). What will be said of you? Will you be found faithful, multiplying the talent entrusted to you (Matthew 25:21)? Or will you be exposed as one who hid your talent in the ground, paralyzed by fear (Matthew 25:25–26)?

This is the final confrontation of identity. This is the dangerous prayer that still burns: "Holy Spirit, show me to me." Not the polished version. Not the rehearsed mask. Show me the man. Show me the woman. Show me the scroll written before time began.

For when you see it, you will never be the same. And when you walk in it, the world will never recover.

Rise, son. Rise, daughter. This is your high calling. This is your anointing. This is your hour.

## Prophetic Decree 1

Do not delude yourself by saying, *"My church is too big to administer the gifts."* That is a lie from the pit. Within moments of the upper room baptism, Peter lifted his voice, and three thousand souls were cut to the heart and believed (Acts 2:41). Days later, he spoke again, and five thousand more were gathered in (Acts 4:4). The numbers exploded beyond ten thousand in mere days, and yet the apostles did not shrink back, did not excuse themselves, did not silence the Spirit.

Yes, there were always voices trying to shut down the gifts and restrain the fire (1 Thessalonians 5:19–20). But the apostles did not tolerate disorder—they simply rebuked the spiritually immature and pressed forward with strong, uncompromising government (Titus 1:5; 1 Corinthians 14:40).

And hear this: they did not have the knowledge, the structures, or the technology you hold today. Still, they governed the outpouring by the Spirit of wisdom and power (Acts 6:3–4). Yet you tell yourself that with one hundred, or one thousand, or even ten thousand people, it is "too large" to administer the gifts publicly. That confession exposes your foundation—it is not Christ the Rock but sand built on fear and human reasoning (Matthew 7:26–27).

If twelve men could steward a revival of multitudes without crumbling, and your leadership cannot manage even a fraction of such a move, then the harvest is not the issue—your leaders are. You need new leaders, equipped by God, not by committees. You need an upgrade in government, a raising up of men and women who can carry Kingdom weight (Exodus 18:21).

Return to the basics! The Kingdom of God is not built on possessions, programs, or polished systems. It is built upon people, living stones set aflame with the Spirit of Christ (1 Peter 2:5). The Kingdom is not in word only but in power (1 Corinthians 4:20). Govern the gifts. Release the fire. Build the people—not the things.

## Prophetic Decree 2

You dare to cut branches from other trees, graft them into yourself, and then burn down the very tree God planted to bear fruit. You trample the calling of another and then attempt to wear it as though it were your own mantle. But hear this: a grafted branch may sprout leaves and even bear a measure of fruit, yet it will never yield the abundance that the original tree—divinely planted and purposed—was destined to produce (John 15:16).

This is what happens when pastors despise the vessel God has chosen because they dislike the "package" in which the gift arrives. Instead of honoring the anointing, they seek to mold another in their own image, duplicating what they prefer. But the Spirit of the Lord does not anoint human preference. He anoints divine assignment (1 Samuel 16:7). No man can reproduce the unique work of God by human devices, strategies, or manipulations (Zechariah 4:6).

You cannot hijack another's call and make it yours. You cannot graft what God never ordained and expect Kingdom fruit. The gifts and callings of God are irrevocable (Romans 11:29). To resist the vessel He has chosen is to resist the Lord Himself (Acts 9:5). Stop scorning the tree He planted. Stop despising the servant He sent. Nurture the field God has given you, and it will yield a harvest far greater than the counterfeit fruit of stolen branches (Matthew 21:43).

**Scripture References:**

- Ephesians 2:10
- 2 Corinthians 4:7

- Romans 11:29
- Judges 13:5

- Judges 16:20
- Judges 16:28
- 1 Samuel 3:1
- 1 Samuel 3:20
- 1 Samuel 7:15
- 1 Samuel 16:14
- Isaiah 42:8
- Proverbs 27:17
- 2 Timothy 1:6
- Romans 11:36
- Psalm 40:7-8
- Hebrews 10:7
- Revelation 20:12
- Matthew 25:21
- Matthew 25:25-26
- Acts 2:41
- Acts 4:4
- 1 Thessalonians 5:19-20
- Titus 1:5
- 1 Corinthians 14:40
- Acts 6:3–4
- Matthew 7:26–27
- Exodus 18:21
- 1 Peter 2:5
- 1 Corinthians 4:20
- John 15:16
- 1 Samuel 16:7
- Zechariah 4:6
- Romans 11:29
- Acts 9:5
- Matthew 21:43

# Glossary of Terms

**Abundant Life (Zoe vs. Bios)**

> Zoe: The God-kind of life, Spirit-empowered and aligned with divine design (John 10:10).

> Bios: Natural, biological life—mere existence without divine overflow.

> Application: Living from Zoe brings joy, creativity, and fulfillment.

> See also: Design, Identity, Worship.

**Agreement**

> Spiritual alignment with God's design that unlocks provision and authority. "Can two walk together unless they are agreed?" (Amos 3:3).

> Application: Destiny requires agreement with Heaven, not with culture.

> See also: Obedience, Scroll, Assignment.

**Anointing**

> The empowerment of the Spirit to fulfill divine calling. The anointing breaks yokes (Isaiah 10:27) and equips for assignment.

> Application: Anointing rests on authenticity, not imitation.

> See also: Mantle, Authority, Legacy.

**Anomaly (The Anomaly Generation)**

>A holy disruptor, set apart to break patterns and establish new Kingdom standards. Elijah was an anomaly to his age (1 Kings 18).

>Application: You are not an alternative—you are the assignment.

>See also: Remnant, Distinction, Prophetic Identity.

**Apostolic Thinking**

>A mindset of building, sending, and discipling nations, not just gathering crowds (Matthew 28:19).

>Application: Apostolic believers reform culture rather than retreat from it.

>See also: Gates, Reformation, Occupy.

**Assignment**

>Your Heaven-given mandate tied to identity. Unlike talent, assignment is eternal (Ephesians 2:10).

>Application: Assignment clarifies priorities and fuels obedience.

>See also: Calling, Scroll, Obedience.

**Authority**

>The right and power to act on Heaven's behalf. Authority flows from submission and identity (Luke 10:19; Romans 5:17).

>Application: True authority changes atmospheres and confronts darkness.

See also: Dominion, Mantle, Voice of the Spirit.

**Spirit of Babylon - (Babylon)**

A demonic system of pride, idolatry, immorality, and rebellion against God that corrupts cultures and enslaves people, symbolizing confusion and captivity; it resists the Kingdom of God and seduces believers into compromise (Revelation 18:2–4).

Application: The satanic influence of deception, lust, and pride that draws people into rebellion against God (Isaiah 47:10–11).

Prophetic Edge:

A demonic power that demands conformity to sin, exalts man above God, and intoxicates nations with corruption and shame (Revelation 17:4–5).

**Calling vs. Competence**

Calling: Identity-based, Heaven's alignment.

Competence: Learned skill that may not match divine purpose (Romans 11:29).

Application: Don't confuse applause for calling.

See also: Assignment, Nature, Design.

**Cloning Spirit**

The pressure to imitate others rather than walk in authentic design. Paul warned against conforming to patterns (Romans 12:2).

Application: Cloning silences uniqueness and kills revival.

See also: Herd Mentality, Distinction, Worship.

## Crown

Symbol of victory, identity, and reward for faithfulness (2 Timothy 4:8; Revelation 3:11).

Application: The crown is not for retreating but for reigning.

See also: Authority, Dominion, Legacy.

## Dangerous Prayer

A bold prayer that demands transformation—"Holy Spirit, redefine me. Show me to me." (Psalm 139:23–24).

Application: Dangerous prayers unlock scrolls and strip false identity.

See also: Identity, Metamorphosis, Discovery.

## Design (Original Design)

Your unique divine blueprint, crafted before birth (Jeremiah 1:5; Psalm 139:14).

Application: Distinction is not dysfunction—it's Heaven's signature.

See also: Nature, Worship, Assignment.

## Destiny Scroll (Book of Destiny)

The heavenly manuscript of your life (Psalm 40:7; Hebrews 10:7). Your life is judged against what was written.

Application: To live undiscovered is to remain a sealed scroll.

See also: Assignment, Prophetic Identity, Legacy.

## Devastation vs. Revelation

God may use failure or crisis to reposition you when you resist His voice (Romans 8:28).

Application: Don't wait for devastation—move by revelation.

See also: Metamorphosis, Seasons, Obedience.

## Distinction

Your divine difference. Being set apart is the mark of divine favor (1 Peter 2:9).

Application: Difference is your weapon against mediocrity.

See also: Anomaly, Remnant, Cloning Spirit.

## Dominion

The mandate to rule and steward creation as sons of God (Genesis 1:28; Romans 5:17).

Application: Dominion is not arrogance; it is alignment.

See also: Authority, Occupy, Kingdom Advancement.

## Gates (Seven Gates of Culture)

Strategic entry points of influence in society (family, government, media, education, economy, religion, arts) (Nehemiah 3).

Application: Reform begins at the gates.

See also: Apostolic Thinking, Reformation, Occupy.

## Garments of Identity

Spiritual coverings that represent identity and authority. "Put on the new man" (Ephesians 4:22–24).

Application: You wear what you believe—truth or residue.

See also: Mantle, Legacy, Metamorphosis.

## Herd Mentality (Spirit of the Herd)

The bondage of blending with the crowd (Exodus 23:2).

Application: The herd follows opinions; the remnant follows revelation.

See also: Cloning Spirit, Remnant, Distinction.

## Hyperbolē

Greek term meaning "to throw beyond" (2 Corinthians 4:7). Refers to the excellence of God's power that surpasses human strength.

Application: God calls you to operate beyond natural limits.

See also: Anomaly, Authority, Prophetic Identity.

## Inheritance

Spiritual legacy and Kingdom resources passed from one generation to the next (Ephesians 1:18).

Application: Inheritance is not what you take but what you steward.

See also: Legacy, Mantle, Scroll.

## Issachar (Sons of Issachar)

A tribe known for discerning times and seasons (1 Chronicles 12:32).

Application: Modern Issachars interpret culture prophetically and align action with timing.

See also: Seasons, Prophetic Identity, Reformation.

## Legacy

Not what you leave but what you launch. Multiplying
mantles, not memorializing them (Proverbs 13:22).

Application: Legacy is generational design in action.

See also: Inheritance, Mantle, Scroll.

## Mantle

A prophetic garment symbolizing calling and authority (1
Kings 19:19; 2 Kings 2:13–14).

Application: Mantles must be multiplied, not memorialized.

See also: Garments of Identity, Legacy, Anointing.

## Metamorphosis

The radical transformation from old man to new creation
(Romans 12:2; Ephesians 4:23–24).

Application: Metamorphosis requires surrender and
renewal.

See also: Dangerous Prayer, Discovery, Worship.

## Nature (Divine Nature)

Your intrinsic, God-given wiring that reveals calling
(Romans 12:6; 2 Peter 1:4).

Application: Nature is the fingerprint of Heaven.

See also: Design, Discovery, Worship.

## Obedience

Immediate, wholehearted response to God's voice.
Delayed obedience is disobedience (1 Samuel 15:22).

Application: Obedience is the gate to authority.

See also: Agreement, Voice of the Spirit, Assignment.

## Occupy

To steward, expand, and hold territory until Christ returns (Luke 19:13).

Application: Occupy means advancing, not retreating.

See also: Dominion, Apostolic Thinking, Kingdom Advancement.

## Prophetic Identity

Living as who God says you are, not who culture defines you to be (Jeremiah 1:5; 1 Peter 2:9).

Application: Identity is prophetic when it becomes a tangible assignment.

See also: Scroll, Metamorphosis, Distinction.

## Prophetic Discovery

The uncovering of identity through divine encounter. Prophecy awakens design, but does not replace discovery (1 Corinthians 13:9; 1 Timothy 1:18).

Application: Revelation must be lived, not just heard.

See also: Dangerous Prayer, Discovery, Voice of the Spirit.

## Remnant

The consecrated minority God preserves to reform culture (Romans 11:5).

Application: The remnant rises when compromise deepens.

See also: Distinction, Anomaly, Reformation.

## Repentance

The door to transformation—turning from sin and false identity into alignment with God's scroll (Acts 3:19).

Application: Repentance is not optional; it is foundational.

See also: Metamorphosis, Obedience, Scroll.

## Reformation

God's process of reshaping culture through Kingdom people (Romans 12:2).

Application: Reformation requires courageous distinction.

See also: Apostolic Thinking, Gates, Remnant.

## Seasons of Life

God-ordained stages that require discernment (Ecclesiastes 3:1).

Application: Clinging to past seasons hinders growth.

See also: Issachar, Discovery, Metamorphosis.

## Separation

Leaving environments that mock your design in order to walk in your scroll (Genesis 12:1).

Application: Separation is permission, not punishment.

See also: Distinction, Obedience, Discovery.

## Submission

Yielding to God's order and authority. Authority flows only from submission (James 4:7).

Application: Submission is not weakness but Kingdom alignment.

See also: Authority, Obedience, Agreement.

**Transformation**

The Spirit-led process of being changed into Christ's image (2 Corinthians 3:18).

Application: Transformation precedes influence.

See also: Metamorphosis, Repentance, Worship.

**Undiscovered Life**

Living without identity alignment—a "form of death worse than dying" (Hosea 4:6).

Application: Discovery is non-negotiable for Kingdom impact.

See also: Scroll, Discovery, Identity.

**Violent Reversal (Kingdom Advancement)**

The Kingdom advances forcefully, reversing darkness with light (Matthew 11:12).

Application: Advancement requires courage, confrontation, and movement.

See also: Dominion, Occupy, Authority.

**Voice of the Spirit**

The clear frequency of Heaven that commissions and confronts (Revelation 2:7; Romans 8:14).

Application: To ignore the Spirit is rebellion, not neutrality.

See also: Obedience, Assignment, Prophetic Discovery.

### Worship Is Design

Worship is not a genre or a song—it is living in alignment with God's design (Romans 12:1).

Application: When you live in your true nature, you are worshipping.

See also: Design, Nature, Assignment.

# Thematic Word Index

183

# Scripture Index

## Old Testament

187

191